the ... ner

...ssential guide

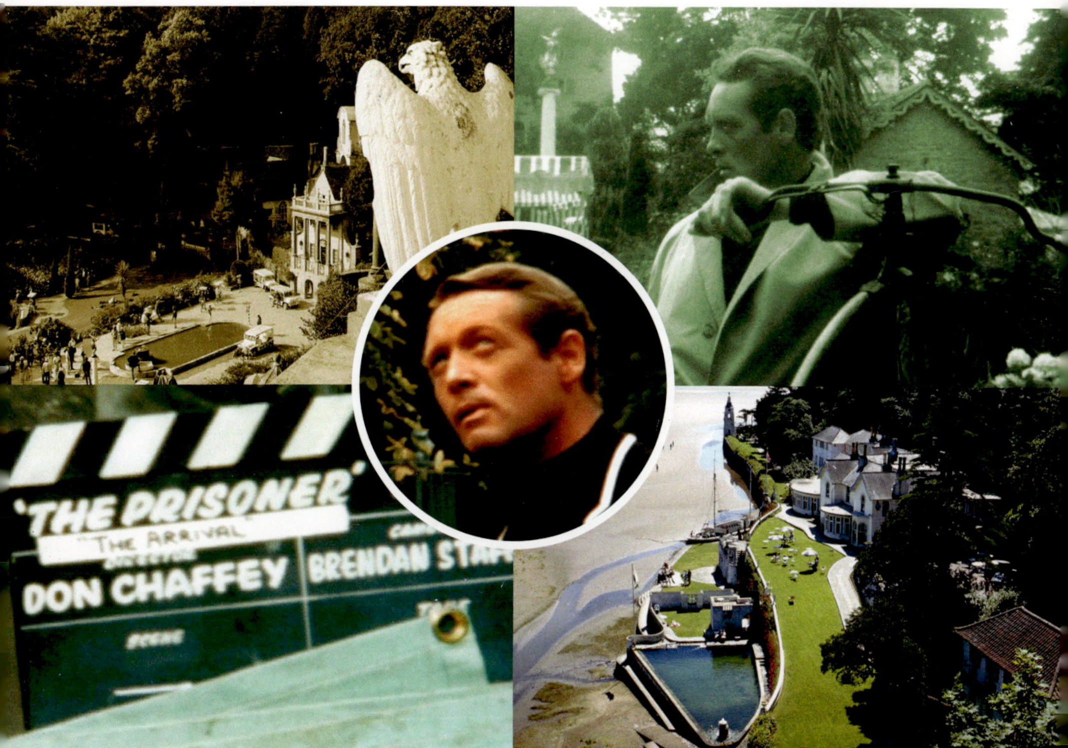

Rick Davy

QUOIT

This edition first published in 2017 by Quoit Media Limited, Brynmawr, Llanfair Caereinion, Powys, SY21 0DG

For more copies of this book, please email quoit@quoitmedia.co.uk

ISBN 978-1-911537-05-2

A CIP catalogue record for this book is available from the British Library

Printed and bound in Great Britain

Designed and edited by Alan Hayes

With thanks to Simon Coward, Steven Ricks, Robert Fairclough and Andrew Pixley for their unrivalled research into *The Prisoner*

Additional thanks to Roger Goodman, Tim Beddows, Nicholas Briggs and everyone who has allowed or licensed their photographs to be included

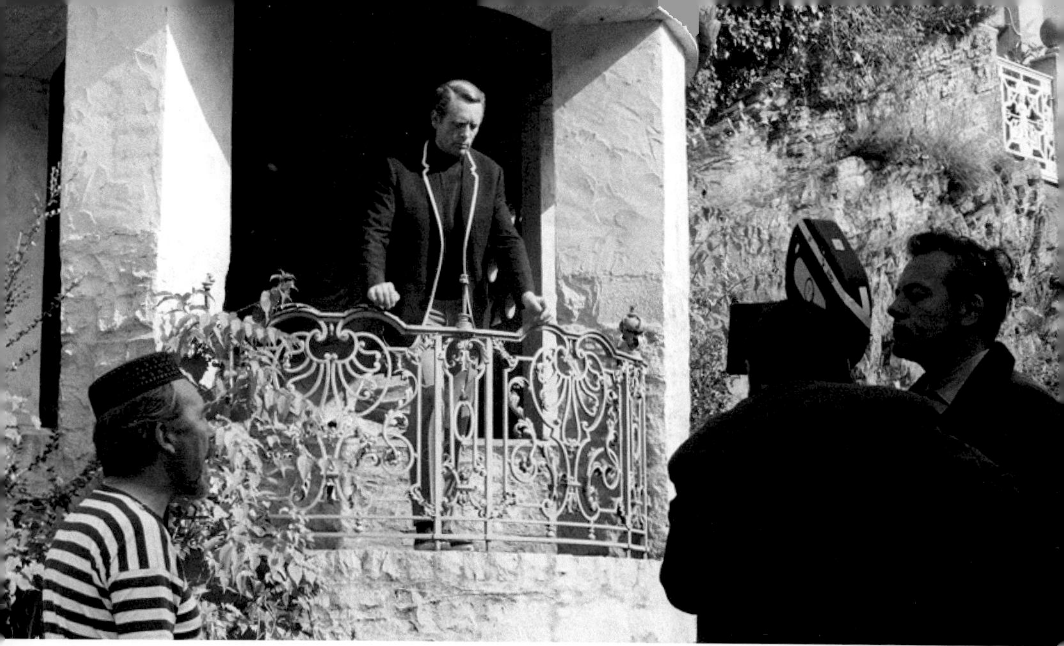

Image © Rick Davy

Introduction

Ask any television historian to list the most influential programmes of all time and most will be sure to mention *The Prisoner*.

Filmed in 1966 and 1967, the 17 episode series is rightly regarded as one of the finest – and most bizarre and controversial – television dramas ever made.

Half a century later, the series continues to entertain and enthral viewers. A fast-paced Bond-like action-adventure series on the one hand and an allegorical conundrum on the other, no other television series, before or since, has asked as many questions and had as great an impact as *The Prisoner*.

The series starred Patrick McGoohan as a man who resigns from a confidential job and is abducted to a strange town, known only as The Village, from which there is no escape. All the 'inmates' of The Village are stripped of their identity and given numbers instead of names (McGoohan played Number Six). They are brainwashed and tortured in a variety of ways to have their knowledge extracted.

Each episode would follow Number Six's attempts to escape, as well as his efforts to determine whether The Village was run by his own side or someone else, and to identify the never-seen, mysterious Number One. Number Two – next in command and each week played by a different guest star actor – would try new and increasingly extreme techniques to ascertain why Number Six had left his job.

The series' production process and conception is as complicated and baffling as some of what we see on screen, and many of the finished elements of the series could be described as serendipitous accidents.

Regardless, it remains to this day one of the most daring and expertly assembled series. With its warning of the dehumanisation of society at its core, coupled with futuristic elements such as credit cards, cordless phones, state control, and covert surveillance, the series was well ahead of its time and is as relevant today as it was when it was conceived.

One Man's Show?

The driving force behind *The Prisoner* was its star, co-creator and executive producer Patrick McGoohan, who also directed and wrote several of the episodes.

Patrick Joseph McGoohan was born on 19th March 1928 (a birthdate shared by his Number Six character) in Queens, New York. His family moved to Ireland when he was a small child, and he later settled in Sheffield, where after a succession of various jobs, he decided to become an actor.

McGoohan quickly established himself as a fine stage actor, with his performance as Ibsen's *Brand* (which was also filmed and screened by the BBC) still held in high esteem today.

A series of increasingly large film and television parts followed, including leading roles in classic films such as *Hell Drivers*, *High Tide at Noon* and *Nor the Moon by Night*, before independent television mogul Lew Grade chanced upon the Clifford Odets TV play *The Big Knife* on 30th December 1958.

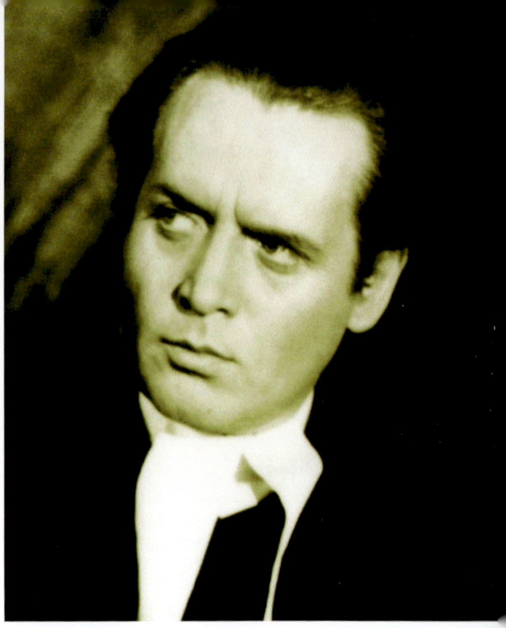

Patrick McGoohan in 1963
© The Disney Channel

Grade was looking for a leading man for his new action adventure series *Danger Man* (shown as *Secret Agent* in the USA). The play's leading man caught his eye, and consequently McGoohan was soon cast as secret agent John Drake.

Drake was no ordinary secret agent; he did not kiss his leading ladies and did not carry a gun, something which McGoohan insisted upon. This moral stance would later lead to McGoohan turning down the role of James Bond.

McGoohan starred in *Danger Man* for six years and 86 episodes but, bored by its increasingly formulaic plots, he 'resigned' his role and approached Grade with a new idea for a TV show.

For many years, McGoohan had been fascinated by the idea of a film or series involving a 'man in isolation', and had discussed the idea with David Tomblin, who had also worked for many years on the *Danger Man* series. The two met and set up the company Keystone Films Limited (later re-named Everyman Films).

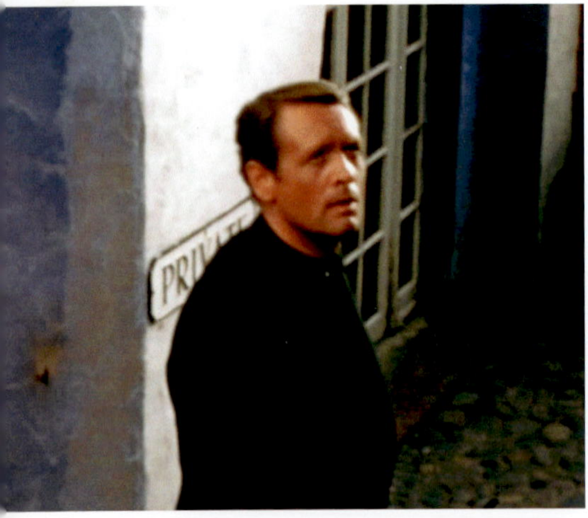

McGoohan filming Arrival at Portmeirion
© Rick Davy

McGoohan presented Lew Grade with a few pages of information about the new series, and some photos of Portmeirion. The two men shook hands (there was never a formal contract) and *The Prisoner* was born.

The question of who created the *Prisoner* series is one which has been debated by historians and fans since the series was first screened.

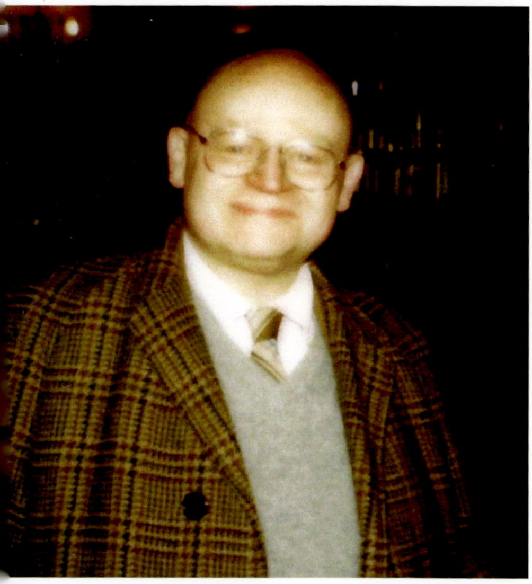

George Markstein
© Eric Mival

Like McGoohan, script editor George Markstein also laid claim to having created the series, maintaining he based it on research he had conducted into World War II establishments, such as Inverlair Lodge in Scotland, where secret agents were held, rested and retrained in secret.

Whilst George Markstein's knowledge of the world of spies, not to mention his familiarity with TV writers (he chose all the *Prisoner* writers), was invaluable, it is clear that it was McGoohan's drive and ideas which changed *The Prisoner* from a very good spy series into an unforgettable allegorical conundrum.

As the series progressed, McGoohan became more and more involved. As well as producing, starring, writing and directing, he was also often present in cutting rooms, directing the editors to create exactly what he wanted, even down to whistling the music that he would like included.

After *The Prisoner* was screened, the McGoohan family moved to Los Angeles, via a short residence in Switzerland.

Patrick McGoohan's career in later years was not as prolific as it had been in the 1960s, but a number of memorable roles would come his way, including several acclaimed appearances in the long running detective series *Columbo*, and an unforgettable appearance as Edward Longshanks in the film *Braveheart* in 1996.

Patrick McGoohan passed away on 13th January 2009 in California, survived by his beloved wife Joan and his three daughters Catherine, Anne and Frances.

Patrick McGoohan, with friend Larry Green, in 2008
© Larry Green

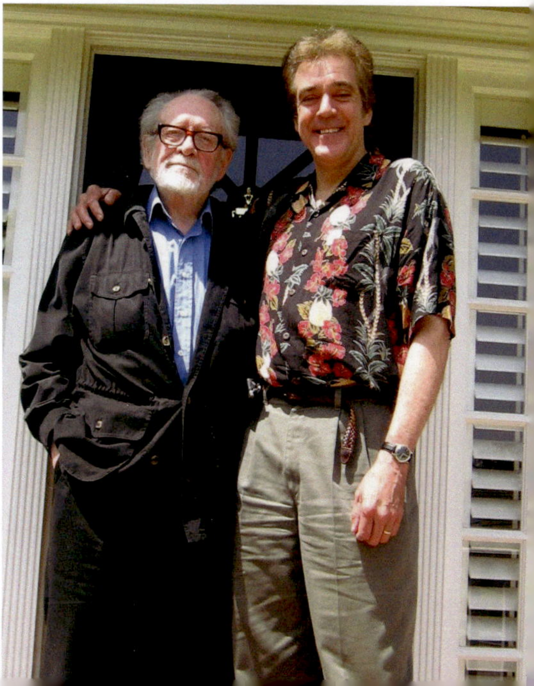

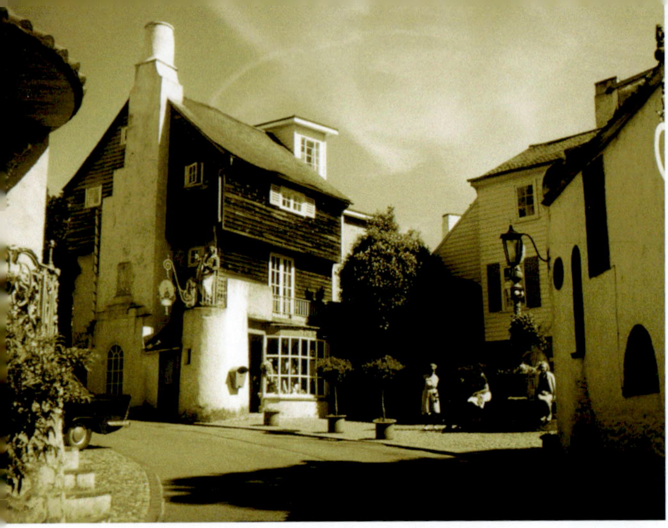

Battery Square in the '60s
© Rick Davy

Portmeirion was the brainchild of architect Sir Clough Williams-Ellis. He wanted to develop a site with the idea that you could place buildings on a natural location without defiling it. After originally intending to buy and build on a small island, Clough purchased from his uncle a site on the North Wales coastline.

The site was originally thick with woodland, and when Williams-Ellis purchased it only four buildings stood (those which are now known as White Horses, Mermaid, Salutation, and the main hotel building).

Originally called Aber Ia (meaning frozen estuary), he renamed the area Portmeirion ('port' as it was by the sea, and 'meirion' due to its location in Merionethshire). Clough officially opened the site as a hotel at Easter 1926, calling it "a holiday retreat for the more discerning."

Choosing The Village

The village of Portmeirion, in Gwynedd, North Wales, was chosen as the setting for The Village in *The Prisoner* by Patrick McGoohan himself. He had previously attended location shooting there for six episodes of *Danger Man* in 1959.

McGoohan later recalled to Chris Rodley for the documentary *Six Into One*, "This was a setting that could be beautiful enough, mysterious enough and confining enough to be the place for our man in isolation."

Lady's Lodge and the Round House
© Rick Davy / Mathew Lock estate

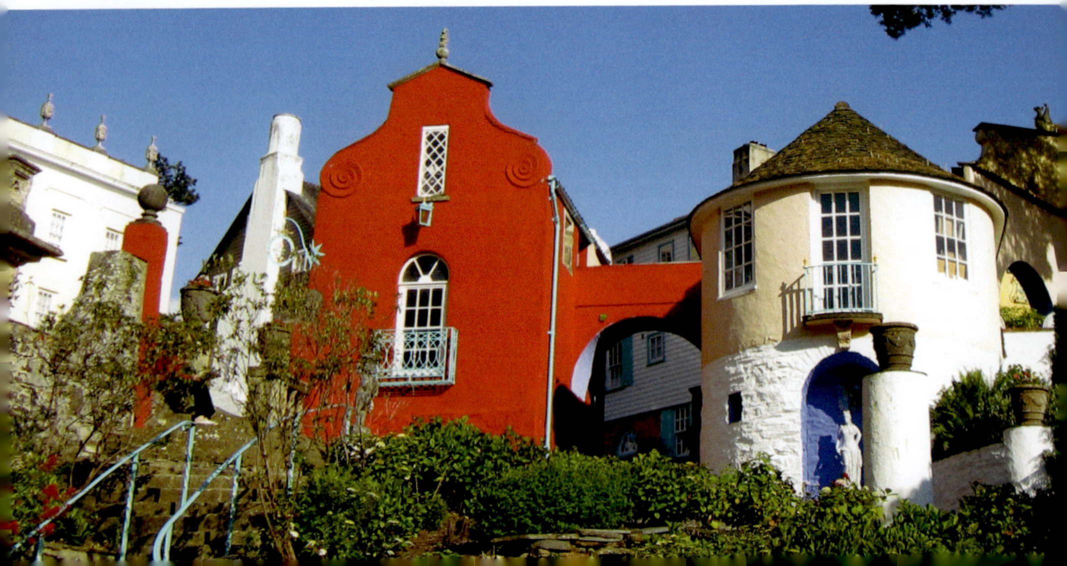

It quickly became so popular that Clough started to vary the prices depending on visitor numbers, so that the fee would increase during busy periods. Regular visitors included Frank Lloyd Wright, Dambuster Guy Gibson, and Noel Coward (who famously wrote the play *Blythe Spirit* during one stay in Fountain cottage).

Over the next fifty years he developed the site, designing and constructing buildings of his own, as well as collecting and reconstructing buildings, statues and architectural curios from all around the world.

He built the site in two phases. The first (1925-1939) saw the erection of buildings such as Angel, Neptune, Chantry and the impressive Campanile bell tower. Building restrictions put in place during World War II then caused construction work at Portmeirion to cease. The second phase commenced in 1954 once these limitations were lifted, and continued until 1976.

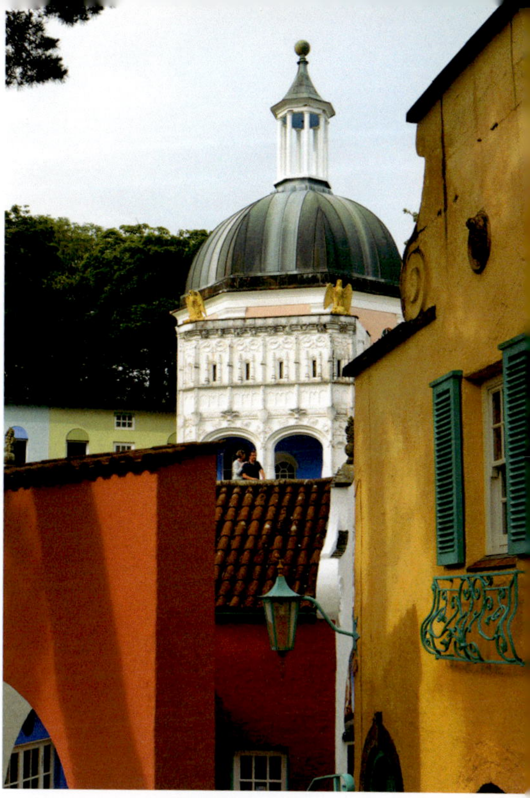

The Dome viewed from Campanile steps

He would call Portmeirion his "Home for fallen buildings" due to his love of rescuing buildings destined for destruction; for example, Hercules Hall was built to house the beautiful ceiling of Emral Hall in Flintshire, and the Bristol Colonnade stood crumbling and decayed in front of a Bristol bath-house until purchased and transported by Sir Clough.

Today, the village is still run by Sir Clough's family, as a hotel complex, with each of the cottages available as nightly serviced or self-catering accommodation, and remains one of Wales' most popular tourist destinations for day visitors. It is also licensed for wedding and civil partnership ceremonies, and each year in September, a music and arts festival, *Festival No. 6*, is held in the village and grounds.

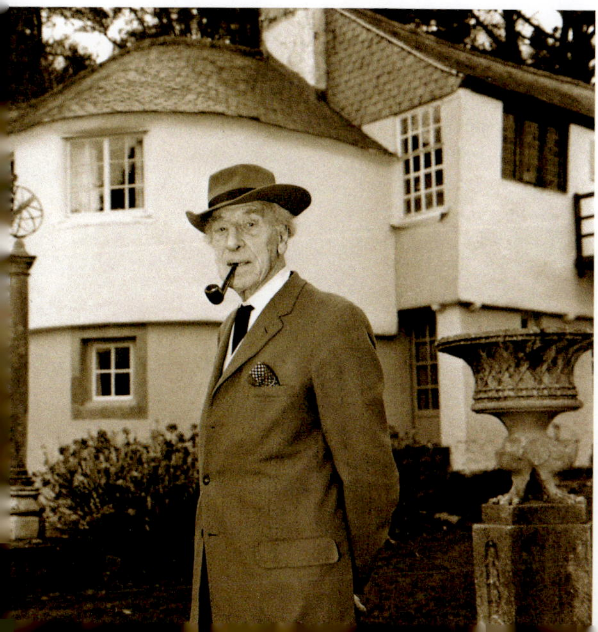

Sir Clough Williams-Ellis

Rover Exposed

One of the most memorable aspects of *The Prisoner* is the sight of the Village guardian, Rover, a giant white balloon-like entity, patrolling The Village and smothering its victims to prevent them from escaping or misbehaving.

Originally, the guardian was to be a much more mechanical device. The original scripts refer to a large patrolling machine with a flashing blue light on top which would hypnotise and control its victims, able to travel across land or sea, and climb walls at high speed.

Such a device was built, and taken to Portmeirion for filming, where it was tested on the road outside of the main hotel building and at the castle.

It was quickly proved to be totally unsuitable, however; the large device, which resembled a go-kart beneath a large black and white peaked cap, was slow, clumsy, noisy, and unable to handle Portmeirion's uneven terrain. There were also problems for the driver, who soon became engulfed with exhaust fumes and was unable to see.

It was clear that a new approach was needed, and quickly, as sequences involving the guardian were to be filmed imminently.

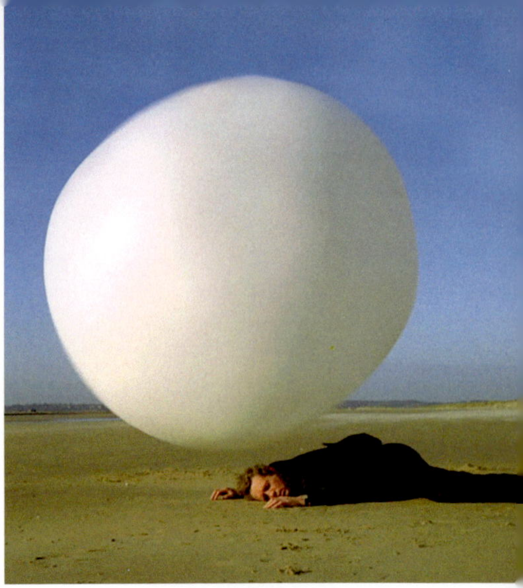

Rover gets its man

There are several conflicting stories as to how the idea of using a balloon came about. Director Don Chaffey stated that he came up with the idea when calling civil servants "a lot of white balloons," while camera operator Ronnie Fox-Rogers, whose job it was to film the underwater and floating Rover sequences, also claimed to have come up with idea – when watching the moving contents of a lava lamp.

Rover being prepared

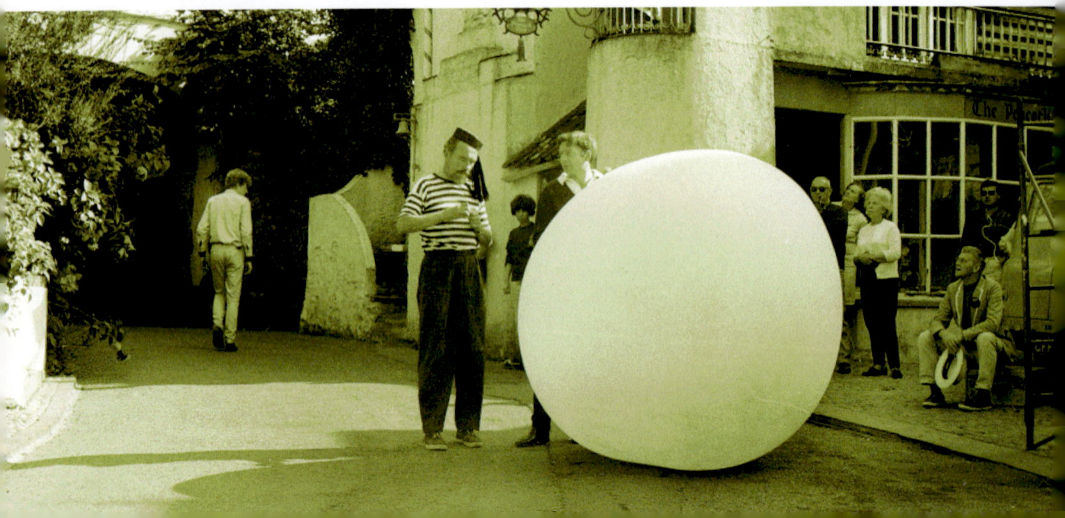

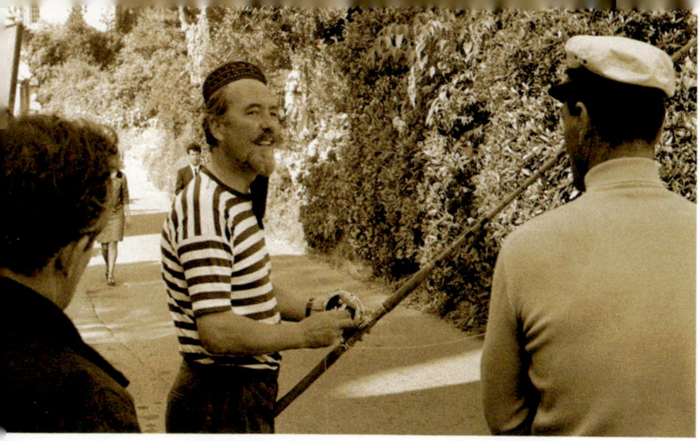

Director Don Chaffey with fishing line
© Rick Davy

The accepted version of events is, however, that by pure chance, production manager Bernie Williams was discussing the failure of the original Rover machine with McGoohan, who looked up at the skies and saw a meteorological balloon floating by. After briefly toying with the idea of using a solid ball, property buyer Sidney Palmer hastily ordered some meteorological balloons to be used in the filming sessions. Several thousand were used during the making of the series.

The balloons were filled with a mixture of air, helium and water to keep them from blowing away too readily. The crew used various clever techniques to 'control' the balloon. These included tying fishing cord from people's legs to the balloons, using a helicopter's downdraft to push them along, and pulling them with wire, often with fishing rods. In some cases, the film would be reversed to make it appear as though the balloon was moving forwards.

Rover's roar was a multi-layered sound effect produced by sound editor Wilf Thompson. He created it by mixing together the sounds of some pellets rolling round a tyre's inner tube, a frogman's breathing apparatus, the slowing down of the sound of a man screaming in a lecture hall, and the playing of a monks' chorus backwards.

Rover is only mentioned by name in one episode, *The Schizoid Man*, and was usually 'launched' with the command of "Orange Alert" from The Village's control room.

The first victim of Rover, in *Arrival*, was played by the 3rd assistant director Seamus Byrne. The effect of Rover seemingly appearing out of nowhere was achieved by propsman Mickey O'Toole shooting a much smaller balloon from the fountain of water with an air gun, before the camera pulled away to reveal the larger balloon.

The balloons often blew away, especially at sea, and it was local man Tecwyn Williams' job to retrieve them, although some did 'escape', leading to calls to the local coastguard! It was never explained on screen what Rover was or how it was powered, but in two episodes (*The Chimes of Big Ben* and *Free For All*) several are shown on screen at once.

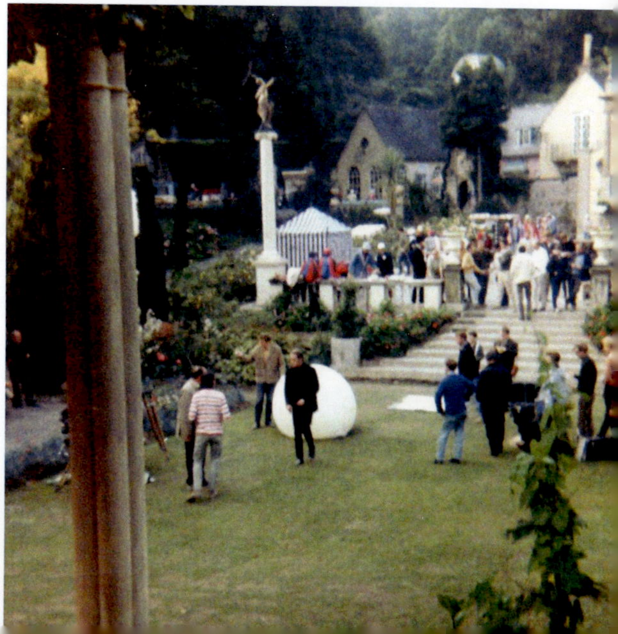

Number Six and his shadow
© Rick Sivyer

The Car's the Star

Lotus Super Seven

Most episodes of *The Prisoner* begin with what is arguably television's most exciting opening title sequence.

A green and yellow Lotus Seven car speeds towards camera down a deserted runway, over Westminster Bridge, and into an underground car park. After resigning his job, the lead character is seen racing home in his car, before he is gassed and abducted as he packs a suitcase.

Originally, ATV wanted Patrick McGoohan's character to drive a Lotus Elan, a car which had appeared in *The Avengers* series, driven by Diana Rigg's Emma Peel character, but in the end McGoohan chose a Lotus Super Seven.

According to Graham Nearn of Lotus, "He was looking for an individual car – something that portrayed this idea of freedom. The word he used was 'maverick'... He saw the Seven in the yard and said: 'That's the car I want.' "

No less than three different Sevens were used during the making of the series. The one seen in the opening sequence and the episode *Many Happy Returns*, registration KAR 120C, was later sold and written off in a racing accident in Australia. The Seven seen in the episode *Do Not Forsake Me Oh My Darling*, using the KAR 120C plate but with actual registration LC K88D, was owned by a resident of Barnet, North London, and loaned to Everyman Films. The third car, featured in the final episode *Fall Out*, and was in fact an earlier Seven which was specially adapted by Nearn and his team to look like a Super Seven.

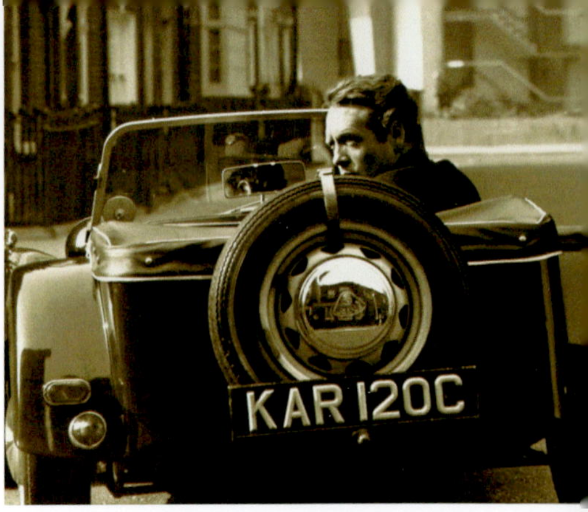

McGoohan with the Super Seven

Stuntman Jackie Cooper drove the Seven at high speed for the runway scene at the start of each episode.

The number plate KAR 120C is now owned by Caterham Cars (the company which Graham Nearn later founded), and Nearn can himself be seen in *Fall Out*, driving the car up to Number Six's London home.

In 1992 a limited edition 'Prisoner Series' Seven was created by Caterham, complete with a dashboard plaque which carried Patrick McGoohan's signature.

Sevens at Buckingham Place

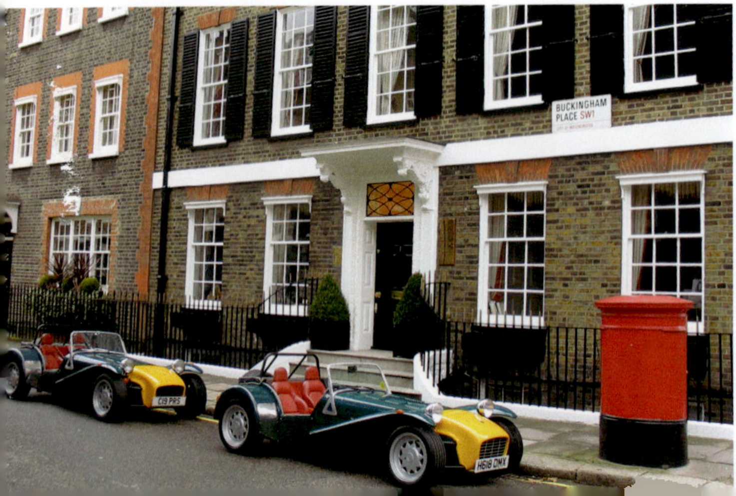

Mini Moke

The distinctive Mini Moke featured in *The Prisoner* as Village taxis. This vehicle was designed by John Sheppard, based on Sir Alec Issigonis' iconic Mini motor car. Originally developed with an eye on the military market, the Moke proved more successful as a road vehicle, with variants produced by both Austin and Morris (and, in later years, by Leyland). The word Moke is a Portuguese word meaning 'donkey'.

Four different Mokes were used during filming, each having its number plate removed and replaced by the word 'taxi', but in the years since the filming of *The Prisoner* only two have ever been found.

For many years, it was believed that the Mini Moke which was parked outside Portmeirion's *The Prisoner Shop* during the 1980s, registration CFC 916C, was one of those used in the series, as it had been used by ITC in promotional photographs, complete with striped canopy. A Moke with registration HLT 790C (which can be briefly seen in one episode with its original number plate on view rather than its 'taxi' plate) was discovered in a barn in Holland in recent years and was sold at auction, in a dilapidated state, for £13,500 in 2015.

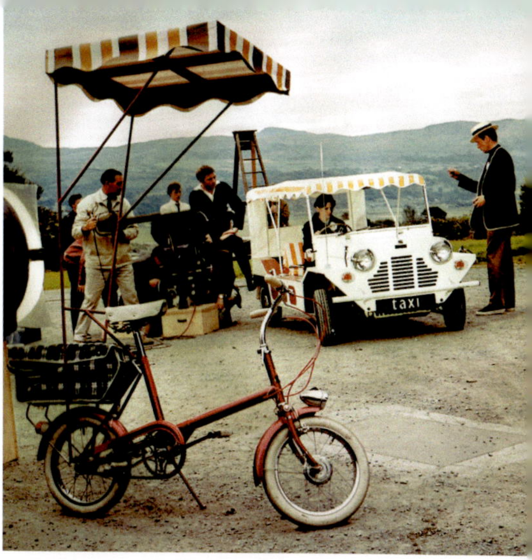

Arrival - Vehicles outside the Hospital
© Roger Goodman

Other Vehicles

The slow moving tractors seen driving the electrics trucks in The Village were adapted Bolens ride-on lawnmowers. The hearse seen at the start of each episode was an Austin Princess Hearse, and the canopied bicycles ridden by Villagers were modified Raleigh RSWs. The Village helicopter was a French-constructed Alouette II helicopter.

The episode *A. B. and C.* features several vehicles, including an Alfa Romeo Giulia Spider and a Citroën DS. In *The Girl Who Was Death*, Number Six drives a Lotus Elan and Sonia an E-Type Jaguar.

Dance of the Dead - Mokes on the Piazza
© Roger Goodman

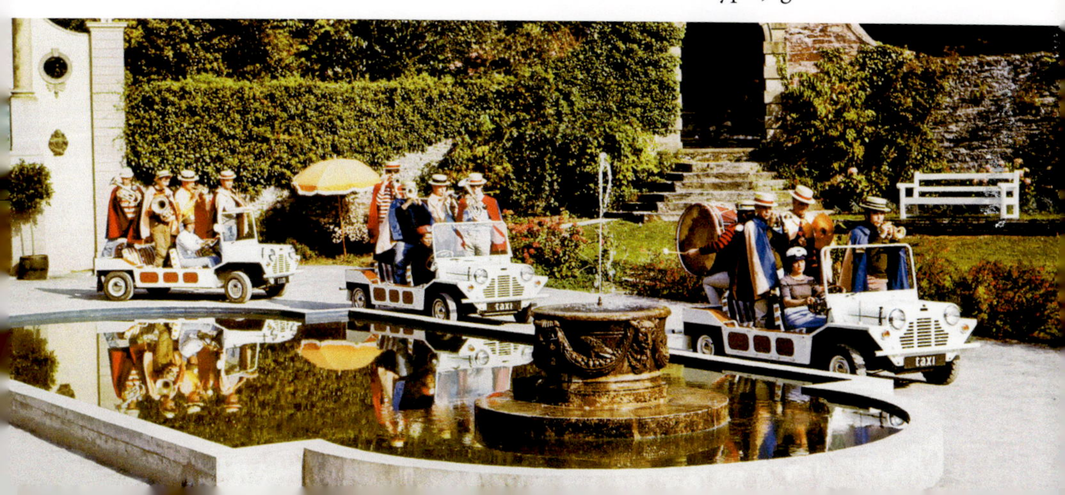

Preparing Portmeirion

In July 1966, original series producer Leslie Gilliat (chosen by Lew Grade as a reliable pair of hands, but who would quit *The Prisoner* that September as he did not share McGoohan's vision for the series) and production manager Bernie Williams visited Portmeirion with hand held film and stills cameras, and shot a short film and a variety of photographs of the location.

In the original script for *Arrival*, Number Two's residence was named as "The Georgian House" (Portmeirion's Unicorn cottage), and there are sequences in the recce film, and still photographs, which confirm the initial importance of this building. In the finished episodes, the character resided within 'The Green Dome' – the imposing Pantheon building.

In 2016, with the uncovering of the original transparency slides from the recce shoot, it was also discovered the Round House, which now houses *The Prisoner Shop*, was likewise not the original choice for Number Six's residence. Instead, Prior's Lodging, a smaller building which sits underneath the Campanile and was used as Number Eight's residence in the episode *The Chimes of Big Ben*, was identified as 'P's House' (P standing for Prisoner) at this pre-production stage.

The central piazza of Portmeirion, which plays an important role in many episodes, was not fully finished when Gilliat and Williams visited. The lines from the tennis court, upon which the pool had been added, are visible in their photographs.

With the location for The Village now confirmed, Portmeirion was prepared, with anything that could give away the true filming location being altered or obscured. Village signage (which was written in 'Village Typeface', a specially adapted version of Albertus) and public

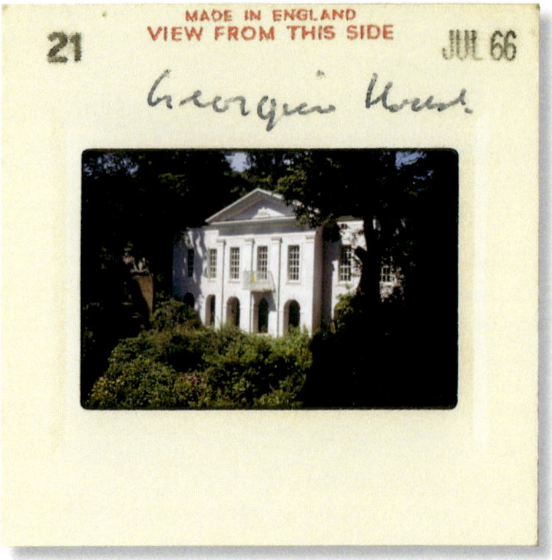

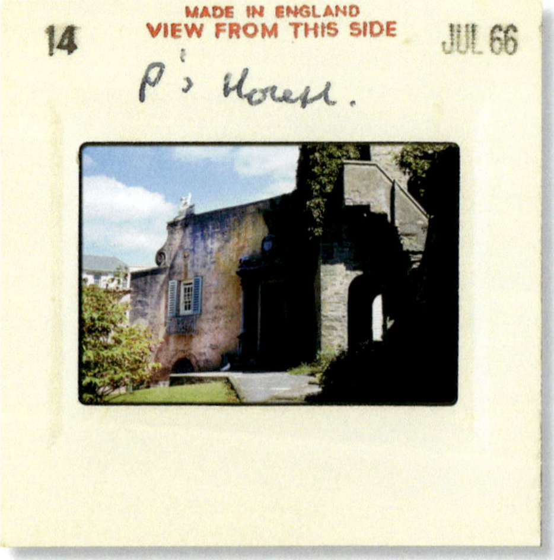

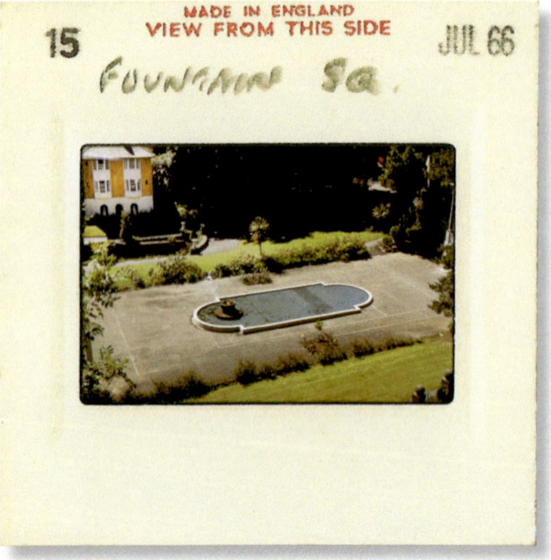

Leslie Gilliat slides © Rick Davy

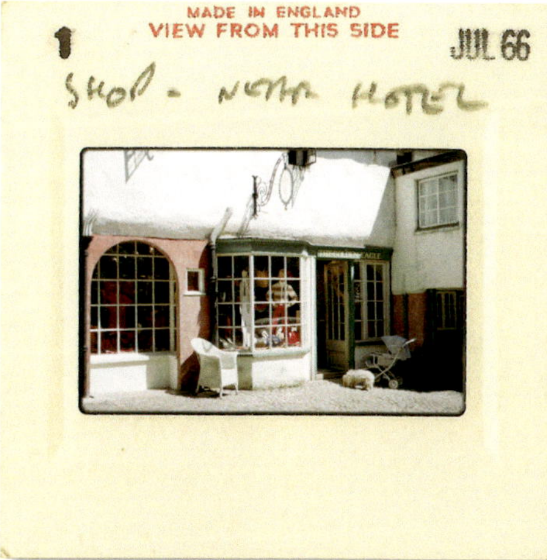

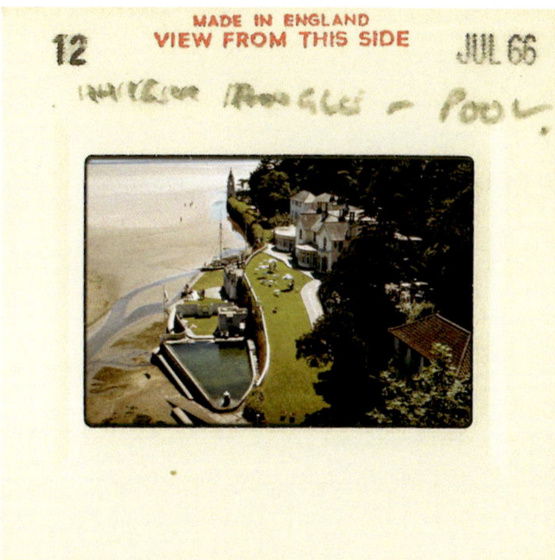

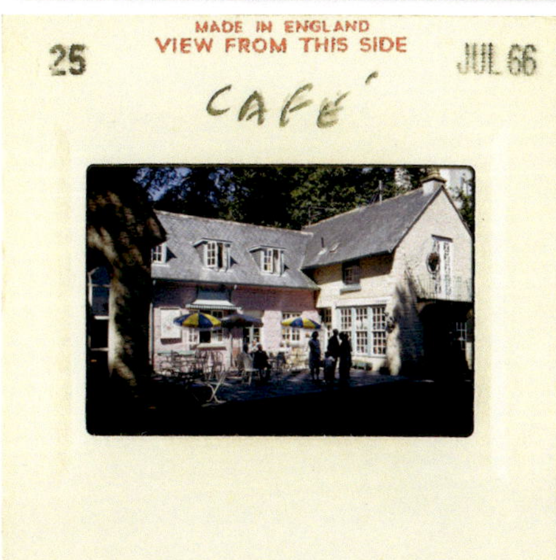

address speakers were added – based on the show's canopied penny farthing motif – and adaptations were made to several buildings (for example, the French windows of the Round House were boarded up). Clever work by directors and camera operators alike made good use of Portmeirion and its buildings, making it look much larger on screen than in reality.

At this early stage, several other buildings had also not been decided upon (with several of the village's shops photographed and labelled). The main hotel building would become the Old People's Home, Castell Deudraeth on the outskirts of the Portmeirion estate the Village hospital, and the Salutation restaurant the Village café.

Patrick McGoohan stayed in the White Horses cottage during filming, with the episode guest stars staying in Watch House and Fountain. The Hercules Hall was occupied by the extras and their costume manager Catherine Williams, with other buildings such as Chantry cottage (make-up and female crew) and Government House (production offices) also being utilised by Everyman Films.

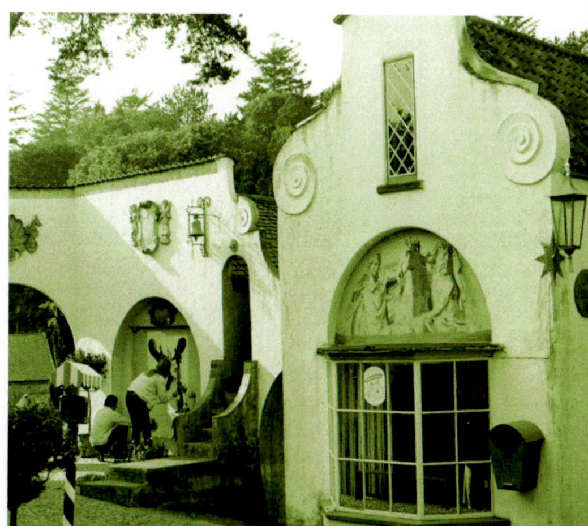

Number Six's house being prepared

© Rick Davy

Extra Special

One of the most important aspects of location filming was to make The Village appear to be heavily populated and, to achieve this effect, local residents were employed as extras.

Porthmadog man Jonathan Jones was given the task of engaging these extras and many locals – a large proportion of whom were recruited via the local telephone exchange – were only too happy to sign up and take part in filming. Many were given important roles which we see on screen and some were even given small speaking parts, including Glyn Jones, who played both a villager and an electrician. However, any extras with strong local accents had their voices re-dubbed so that viewers would not be able to realise that Number Six's exotic prison was actually in Wales. The extras were paid £2 10s per day.

Surprisingly, Portmeirion was kept open during filming and in some behind-the-scenes production shots it is clear that many hundreds of holidaymakers were viewing the filming as it was taking place.

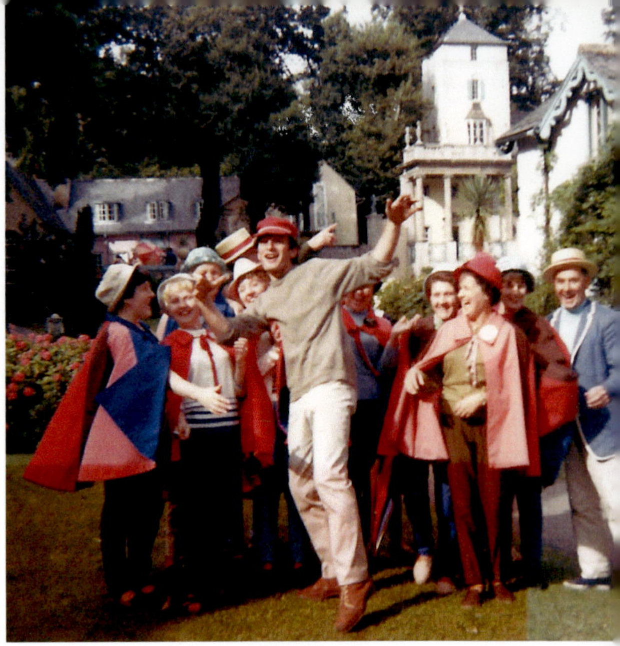

The Telephone Exchange Gang

© Pam McLaughlin

To control the extras and ensure that crowd scenes went according to plan, several crew members were dressed in Village attire so that they could be at the heart of the action and direct the extras. Uncredited assistant director John O'Connor was one of those who fulfilled this role, and he can be seen in many sequences.

Local extras Harold and Marjorie Beer also provided their boat for filming. The *Breda*, which 25 years earlier had taken part in the evacuation of Dunkirk in World War II, was filmed off the coast of Abersoch as MS *Polotska* in the episode *Checkmate* and again as the gun

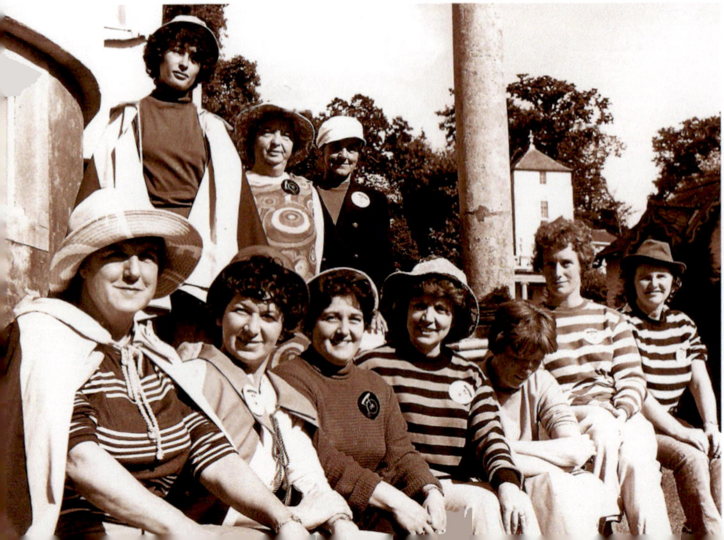

Villagers ready for filming

© Y Cymro / Leri Roberts

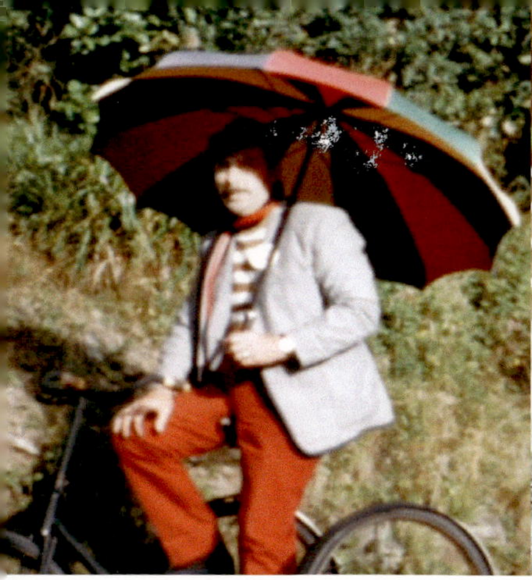

Villager Glyn Jones
© Rick Davy

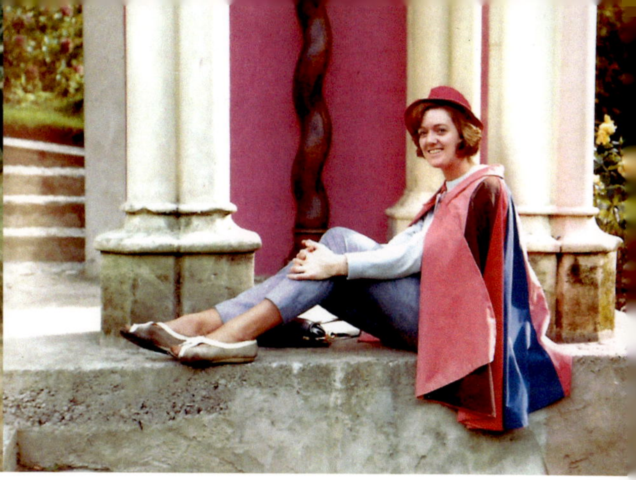

All cloaked up
© Pam McLaughlin

runners' boat in *Many Happy Returns*. The boat remains in operation today.

The town of Porthmadog (some three miles north west of Portmeirion) also played a further part in the series' production. The Coliseum Cinema in the town was where Patrick McGoohan and the rest of the crew would assemble each evening to view the previous day's filming 'rushes'. It was sadly demolished in 2016.

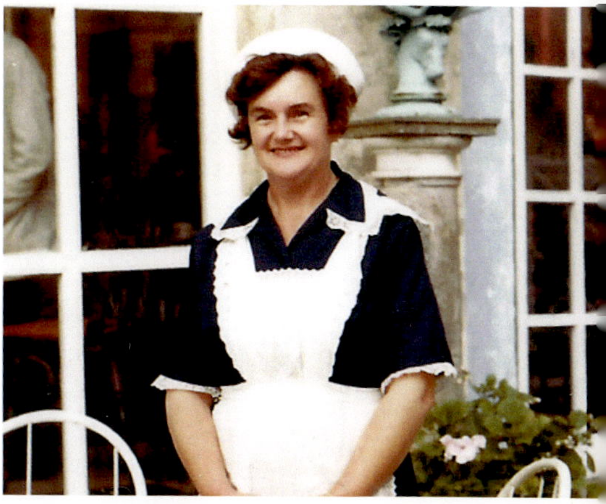

Waitress Megan Jones
© Pam McLaughlin

Extras were also employed back at MGM Studios for the interior scenes. Some actors had early appearances in uncredited roles, such as Roger Lloyd Pack (*Only Fools and Horses*) and comedian Mike Reid (*EastEnders*), who appeared in the episodes *It's Your Funeral* and *Fall Out* respectively.

There have been several occasions when extras involved in the filming have come together again in Portmeirion, including in 1988 and again in 2000, to reminisce about their experiences.

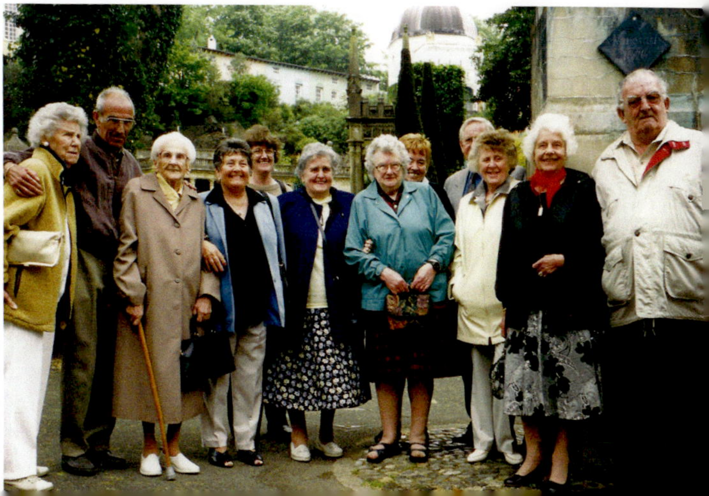

Friends Reunited in 2000
© Robert Fairclough

The Prisoner in Production

The Prisoner was at the time the most expensive TV series ever made (at £75,000 per episode, approximately £1.5m in today's money) and Patrick McGoohan Britain's highest paid TV actor.

After a basic series/writers' guide was created, script editor George Markstein approached and engaged several writers. A batch of scripts was readied during the summer of 1966, with Markstein co-writing the first episode with producer David Tomblin. Most of the crew who had been working with McGoohan, Tomblin and Markstein at the end of *Danger Man* moved straight onto *The Prisoner*, including McGoohan's stunt double Frank Maher.

Filming began in August 1966 with the shooting in London of the opening title sequence, before the crew headed to Portmeirion, with filming at the location commencing on Monday 5th September 1966 and continuing until 29th September.

Movie director Don Chaffey was originally chosen to direct the series, but he and McGoohan disagreed on the approach taken and Chaffey did not direct much more beyond the initial location filming.

During the September of 1966, footage for the episodes *Arrival*, *Free For All*, *Dance of the Dead* and *Checkmate* (plus a small amount for *The Chimes of Big Ben*) was shot. The remaining studio-heavy episodes had to rely on replica sets of The Village and 'stock' shots.

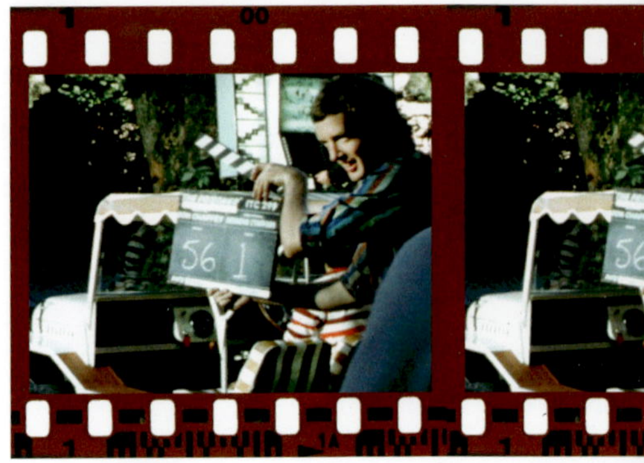

Portmeirion filming - Arrival

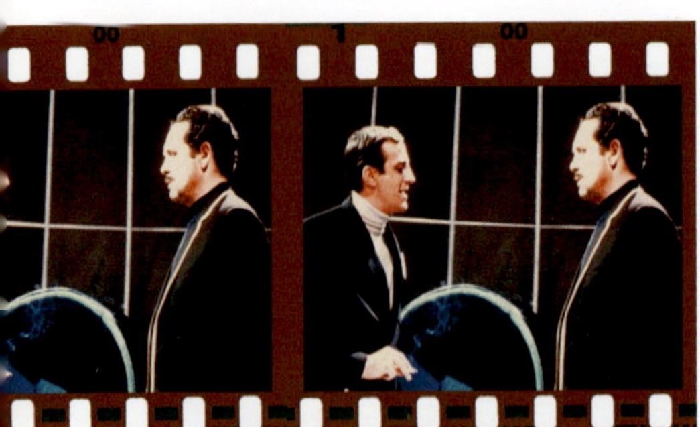

In the Studio - The Schizoid Man

Art Director Jack Shampan was commissioned to design the interior sets for the series, and Ron Grainer (best known at that time for having composed the signature tunes for *Steptoe and Son* and *Doctor Who*) produced a memorable and impactful theme for the series, after previous attempts by fellow composers Robert Farnon and Wilfred Josephs had been rejected. Albert Elms composed some new incidental music, and Chappell's music library was also utilised.

It was decided that each week should see a change of Number Two, and therefore very few recurring roles were created. Maltese actor Angelo Muscat was cast as the mute dwarf butler, despite the original script describing the character as tall and athletic, and Peter Swanwick hired to play a regular Supervisor role. Two voice artistes were also engaged on a regular basis: Fenella Fielding (more famous for her acting roles, such as in *Carry on Screaming*) as the female Village announcer, and Robert Rietti for the male voice-only parts.

Very few guest stars actually attended Portmeirion filming, with only four Number Two actors (Eric Portman, Mary Morris, Rachel Herbert and Guy Doleman) doing so.

Studio filming for the episodes began on Monday 2nd October 1966 and continued for more than a year.

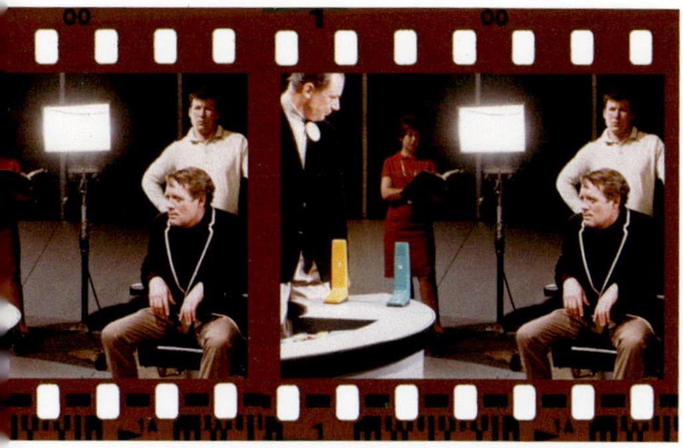

In the Studio - Hammer into Anvil
© QML

The crew returned to Portmeirion in March 1967 to film sequences for the later episodes in the series, most notably *Many Happy Returns* and *Hammer into Anvil*, with stuntman Frank Maher doubling for McGoohan in most sequences.

It became clear early on in production that the television networks in the USA, such as CBS, did not feel the series would be as popular as *Danger Man* had been, and so it was quickly decided that only 17 episodes should be made, rather than the more usual 13, 26 or 39, and that it would be sold abroad as a 'summer filler' rather than a primetime winter series.

As the series' production progressed, the atmosphere around the studio became tense. Directors were regularly replaced as McGoohan took control of more elements of the production, which was both behind schedule and over budget.

McGoohan's increasing desire to add allegory and surreal elements to the series did not sit well with George Markstein, who wanted a more straightforward spy thriller, so Markstein quit *The Prisoner* after the first 13 episodes were completed. With Markstein and his writing contacts gone, McGoohan turned to writers of previous episodes and series crew to provide scripts and ideas for the final four episodes.

After a short production break, the final four episodes were made with a largely new crew, assembled at short notice, and have a different feel to those made previously.

Patrick McGoohan allegedly wrote the final episode, *Fall Out*, in 36 hours, and sets from the previous episode to be filmed, *The Girl Who Was Death*, were reused.

Production on these last four episodes was a frenetic and sometimes stressful experience for the crew, with filming completed at breakneck speed as their transmission dates approached. *Arrival* had its UK premiere on September 29th 1967 on ATV Midlands, to high viewing figures but mixed reviews. The series conclusion was due to air January 19th 1968, but, with location filming in London still taking place in November 1967 and editing still being done the following January, the final two episodes of *Danger Man* were shown instead to give the editors more time, meaning that viewers had to wait until the first week of February 1968 to see *Fall Out*.

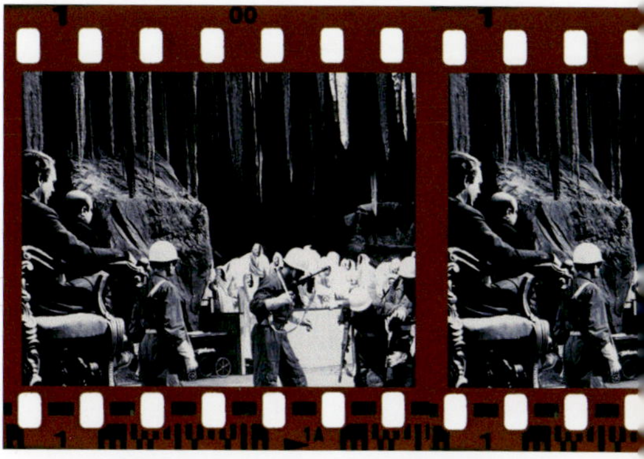

On the Cavern set - Fall Out
© QML

On Location

Whilst a great deal of what we see on screen appears to be Portmeirion, much of the action takes place on studio sets created at MGM Studios in Borehamwood, Hertfordshire. All the interior sequences were filmed there, and several standing sets and Portmeirion-like backdrops were created to match the Village exteriors.

Existing backlot sets on the land behind the studio were also used, with a set created for the film *Eye of the Devil* utilised as the Exhibition Hall in *The Chimes of Big Ben* and the town of Harmony in *Living in Harmony*, with other backlot streets used in episodes such as *A. B. and C.* and *The Girl Who Was Death*.

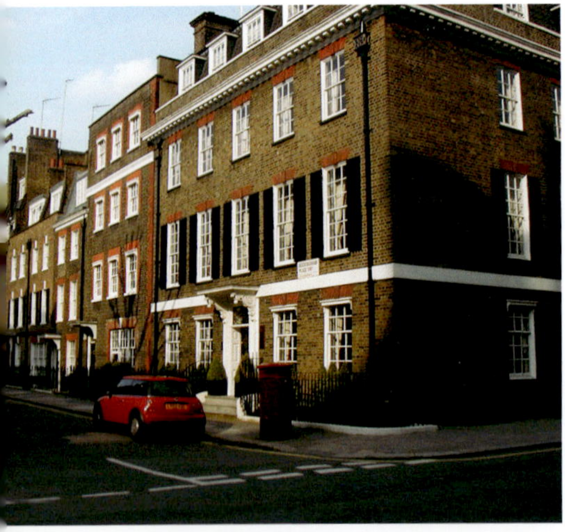

Number Six's London home
© Rick Davy

Filming also took place further afield. The opening sequence begins with the runway shot, filmed at Podington Raceway ('Santa Pod') in Northamptonshire, and then Number Six is seen driving his Lotus in several central London areas, including Westminster Bridge and Abingdon Street car park. The corridor he strides down is situated in a different car park underneath

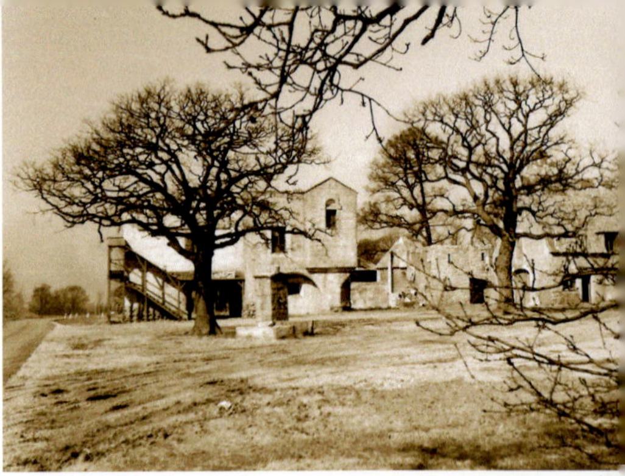

The Harmony set on the MGM backlot
© Eric Mival

Hyde Park. He returns home, via Park Lane and The Mall, to his home at 1, Buckingham Place, Victoria.

Many Happy Returns, *Do Not Forsake Me Oh My Darling* and *Fall Out* also included extra location filming in London.

Some episodes also featured other location shooting, including *The Girl Who Was Death*, which included scenes filmed at the Kursaal and Battersea funfairs, the Beachy Head lighthouse (which also appeared in *Many Happy Returns*), no less than four different venues for the cricket match at the start of the episode (including Bearsted and Meopham in Kent, and Eltisley in Cambridgeshire), in addition to several sequences filmed in the Borehamwood area, near to the studios.

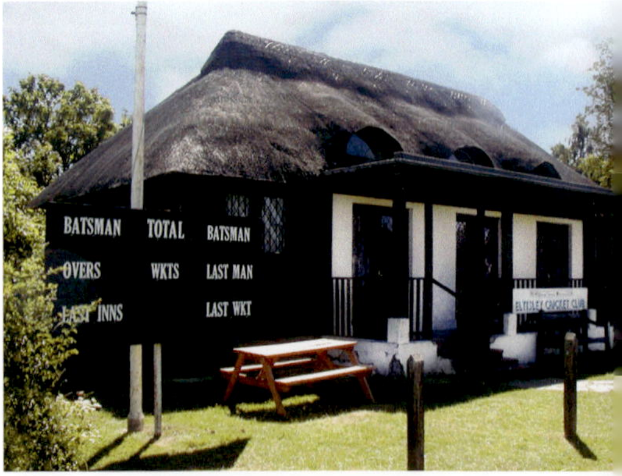

Eltisley Cricket Pavilion
© Rick Davy

The Episodes

The Prisoner

Starring

Patrick McGoohan as *The Prisoner*
Angelo Muscat as *The Butler*

Arrival

Written by George Markstein & David Tomblin
Directed by Don Chaffey

First UK Transmission: 29th September 1967

A man resigns from his job only to be abducted and imprisoned in a strange village from which there is no escape. Known only as Number Six, he meets old friends and new and bids to escape.

Cast

Guy Doleman (*Number Two*), George Baker (*The New Number Two*), Virginia Maskell (*The Woman*), Paul Eddington (*Cobb*), Barbara Yu Ling (*Taxi Driver*), Stephanie Randall (*Maid*), Jack Allen (*Doctor*), Fabia Drake (*Welfare Worker*), Denis Shaw (*Shopkeeper*), Oliver MacGreevy (*Electrician / Gardener*), Frederick Piper (*Ex-Admiral*), Patsy Smart (*Waitress*), Christopher Benjamin (*Labour Exchange Manager*), Peter Swanwick (*Supervisor*), David Garfield (*Hospital Attendant*), Peter Brace*, Keith Peacock* (*Guardians*) George Markstein** (*Man Behind Desk*), William Lyon Brown** (*Undertaker*), Seamus Byrne** (*Rover Victim*), Megan Jones** (*Village Waitress*)

Information

- Actress Patsy Smart, the first person in the series to speak, was the sister of Ralph Smart – creator/producer of *Danger Man*.
- George Baker's Number Two character was the only Number Two in the series to wear a Number Six-style blazer with white piping.
- In the helicopter tour of The Village, Villa Winch cottage has no roof as it was still being built, and the cars of several hotel guests can be seen parked behind the dome.

The Chimes of Big Ben

Written by Vincent Tilsley
Directed by Don Chaffey

First UK Transmission: 6th October 1967

A new arrival who claims to know the location of The Village leads to Number Six using the Village arts and crafts festival as a cover for a new escape attempt.

Cast

Leo McKern (*Number Two*), Nadia Gray (*Nadia*), Finlay Currie (*General*), Richard Wattis (*Fotheringay*), Kevin Stoney (*Colonel J.*), Christopher Benjamin (*Number Two's Assistant*), David Arlen (*Karel*), Peter Swanwick (*Supervisor*), Hilda Barrie (*Number 38*), Jack Le White, John Maxim and Lucy Griffiths (*Judges*)

Information

- For the coastline scenes with David Arlen, Nadia Gray and McGoohan were doused with water from buckets to give the appearance of having just swum to shore.

Alternative Edits

Early versions of both *Arrival* and *The Chimes of Big Ben* have been uncovered in recent years. These contain marked differences to the finished episodes, including alternative credit sequences, music and additional footage.

Both are included on the Network Blu-ray and DVD editions of the series.

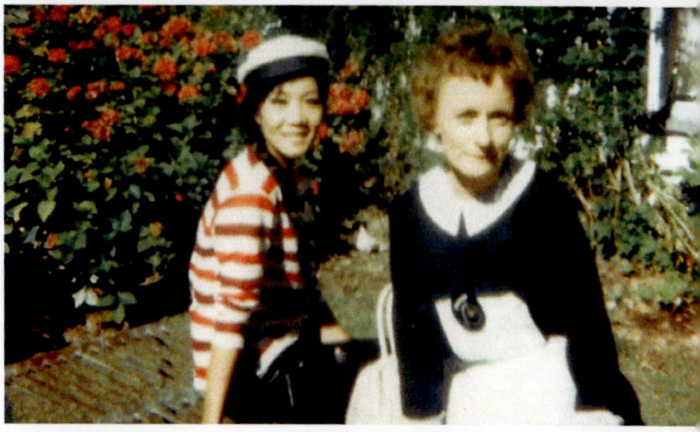

Arrival - Barbara Yu Ling and Patsy Smart
© Pam McLaughlin

All transmission dates are as per the ATV Midlands ITV region, unless stated.
*Actor credited but does not appear / **Uncredited

A. B. and C.

Written by Anthony Skene
Directed by Pat Jackson

First UK Transmission: 13th October 1967

The Village has developed a drug which enables the manipulation of dreams. The new Number Two decides to use it on Number Six to find out why he resigned.

Cast

Colin Gordon (*Number Two*), Katherine Kath (*Engadine*), Sheila Allen (*Number Fourteen*), Peter Bowles (*'A'*), Georgina Cookson (*Blonde Lady*), Annette Carrell (*'B'*), Lucille Soong (*Flower Girl*), Bettine Le Beau (*Maid at Party*), Terry Yorke, Peter Brayham (*Thugs*), Bill Cummings (*Henchman*)

Information

- The episode was originally written under the title 'Play in Three Acts', and was later retitled '1, 2, and 3'.
- Annette Carrell, who played B, sadly died before this episode was screened.
- When Channel 4 broadcast the episode in 1983, they screened a print which had most of the 'B' sequence removed, leading to much confusion for viewers.

Free For All

Written by Patrick McGoohan (as Paddy Fitz)
Directed by Patrick McGoohan

First UK Transmission: 20th October 1967

It's election time in The Village, and Number Six decides to run for the position of Number Two.

Cast

Eric Portman (*Number Two*), Rachel Herbert (*Number 58*), George Benson (*Labour Exchange Manager*), Harold Berens (*Reporter*), John Cazabon (*Man in Cave*), Dene Cooper (*Photographer*), Kenneth Benda, Peter Swanwick** (*Supervisors*), Holly Doone (*Waitress*), Peter Brace, Alf Joint (*Mechanics*)

Information

- McGoohan wrote *Free For All* under the pseudonym Paddy Fitz (Paddy short for Patrick, Fitz after his mother's maiden name Fitzpatrick).
- Number Two actor Eric Portman was quite ill by this time in his life and had to shoot much of his location dialogue in Portmeirion line by line with the help of a prompter.

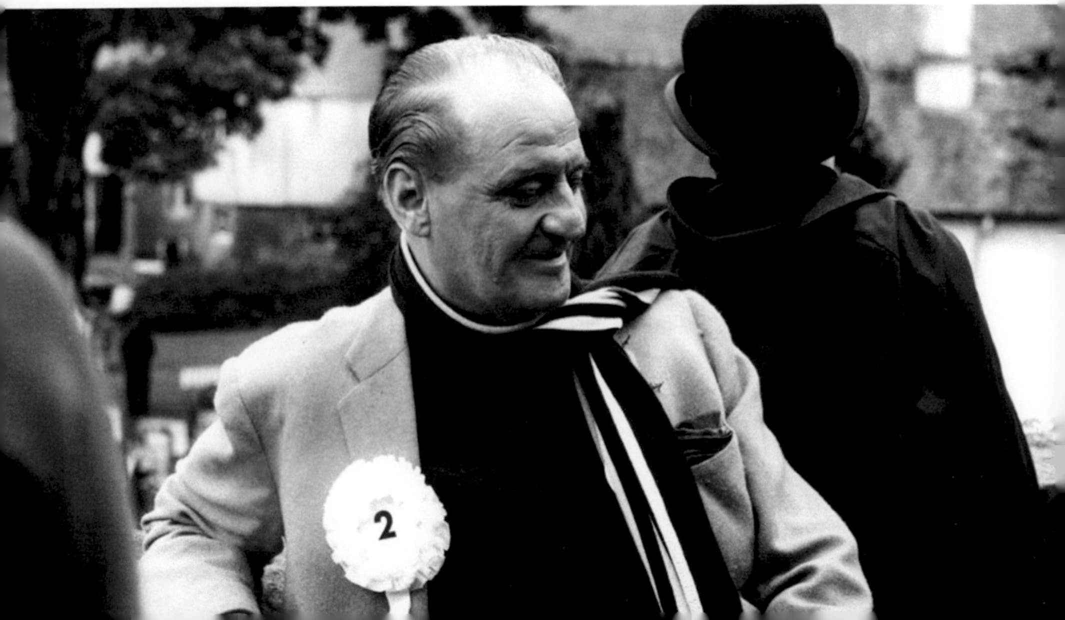

Eric Portman relaxes between takes
© Y Cymro / Leri Roberts

The Schizoid Man

Written by Terence Feely
Directed by Pat Jackson

First UK Transmission: 27th October 1967

Number Six awakens to find he is the new Number Twelve and, in an ingenious Village plan to make him crack, a perfect double of him is now living in his cottage as Number Six.

Cast

Anton Rogers (*Number Two*), Patrick McGoohan (*Number Twelve*), Jane Merrow (*Alison*), Earl Cameron (*Supervisor*), Gay Cameron (*Number 36*), David Nettheim (*Doctor*), Pat Keen (*Nurse*), Gerry Crampton, Dinny Powell (*Guardians*)

Information

- Jane Merrow was cast in this episode as she had previously worked well with McGoohan in four *Danger Man* episodes.
- Originally, Alison was to have identified the real Number Six by kissing the two men, a scene which McGoohan insisted be removed.
- This episode's split screen sequences were filmed with stuntman Frank Maher playing both roles – unseen – opposite McGoohan.

The General

Written by Lewis Greifer (as Joshua Adam)
Directed by Peter Graham Scott

First UK Transmission: 3rd November 1967

Speed Learn, a new way of learning extensive information in a matter of seconds, has taken The Village by storm, but Number Six is an unwilling student and aims to stop it with the aid of a young ally.

Cast

Colin Gordon (*Number Two*), John Castle (*Number Twelve*), Peter Howell (*Professor*), Al Mancini (*Announcer*), Betty McDowall (*Professor's Wife*), Peter Swanwick (*Supervisor*), Conrad Phillips (*Doctor*), Michael Miller (*Man in Buggy*), Keith Pyott (*Waiter*), Ian Fleming (*Man at Café & First Top Hat*), Norman Mitchell (Mechanic), Peter Bourne (*Projection Operator*), George Leech, Jackie Cooper (*Corridor Guards*)

Information

- Writer Lewis Greifer wrote this episode under the pseudonym of Joshua Adam (Joshua and Adam being the names of his two sons).
- Director Peter Graham Scott was called in at short notice by McGoohan to direct *The General* because, according to Scott, "I was quick and I was cheap."

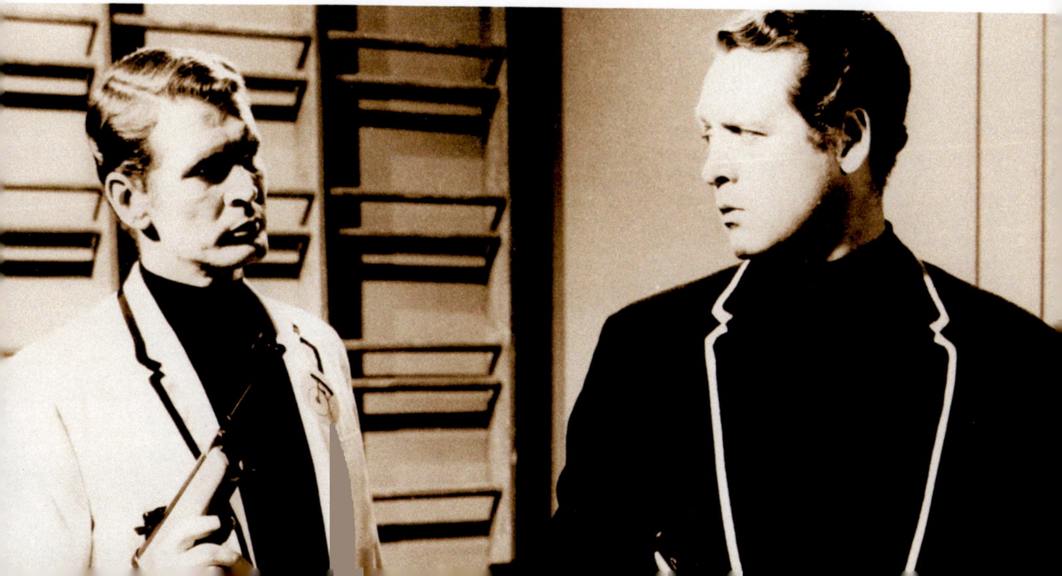

The Schizoid Man - Seeing Double

Many Happy Returns

Written by Anthony Skene
Directed by Patrick McGoohan (as Joseph Serf)

First UK Transmission: 10th November 1967

Number Six awakens to find The Village deserted. He builds a raft to escape back to London, but finds that all is not as he left it.

Cast

Donald Sinden (*The Colonel*), Patrick Cargill (*Thorpe*), Georgina Cookson (*Mrs Butterworth*), Brian Worth (*Group Captain*), Richard Caldicot (*Commander*), Dennis Chinnery (*Gunther*), Jon Laurimore (*Ernst*), Nike Arrighi (*Gypsy Girl*), Larry Taylor (*Gypsy Man*), Grace Arnold (*Maid*), George Markstein** (*Man Behind Desk*)

Information

- The cat which appears in this and the next episode was called Tammy and belonged to locals Catherine and Doug Williams.

- Michael Truman, the original director of *Many Happy Returns*, fell ill and was replaced by McGoohan (directing as Joseph Serf).

Unused Scripts

Several scripts written for the series were not used, including *Don't Get Yourself Killed* by *Checkmate* writer Gerald Kelsey and *The Outsider* by Moris Farhi. Experienced writers Donald Tosh, David Whitaker and others, along with several crew members, including Eric Mival, Tony Sloman and John O'Connor, also suggested storylines which were rejected.

Dance of the Dead

Written by Anthony Skene
Directed by Don Chaffey

First UK Transmission: 17th November 1967

It is carnival time in The Village, but, when Number Six finds a dead body washed up on the beach, he chances upon an opportunity to contact the outside world.

Cast

Mary Morris (*Number Two*), Duncan MacRae (*The Doctor*), Norma West (*Girl Bo-Peep*), Aubrey Morris (*Town Crier*), Bee Duffell (*Psychiatrist*), Camilla Hasse (*Day Supervisor*), Alan White (*Dutton*), Michael Nightingale (*Night Supervisor*), Patsy Smart (*Night Maid*), Denise Buckley (*Maid*), George Merritt (*Postman*), John Frawley (*Flowerman*), Lucy Griffiths (*Lady in Corridor*), William Lyon Brown (*2nd Doctor*), Roy Cannon** (*Dead Body*), Jill Fennessy** (*Girl in Photo*)

Information

- McGoohan hated the first cut of this episode and ordered it to be shelved. Editor John S Smith saw it, re-edited it to McGoohan's satisfaction, and *Dance of the Dead* was saved.

- Trevor Howard was originally cast as Number Two in this episode, and was scripted to have been dressed as Jack the Ripper for the carnival scenes.

Dance of the Dead - Mind Control
© QML

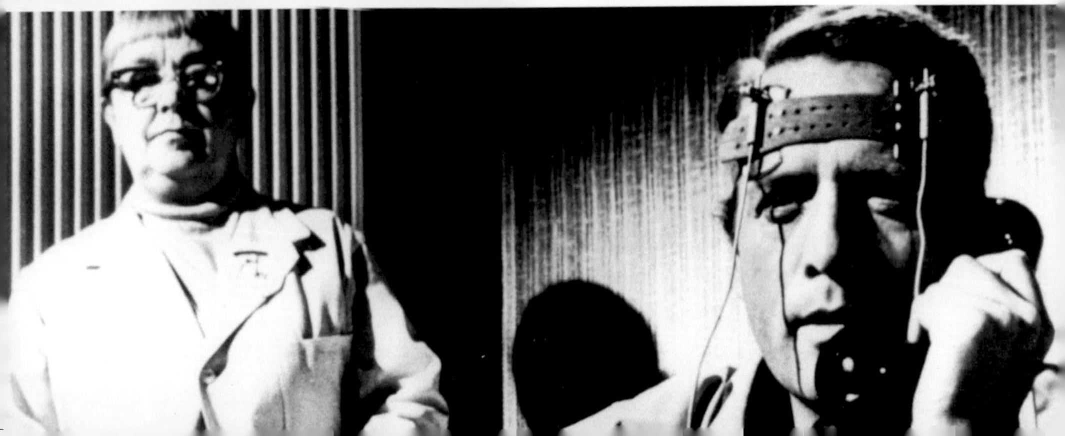

Checkmate

Written by Gerald Kelsey
Directed by Don Chaffey

First UK Transmission: 24th November 1967

Number Six devises an ambitious escape plan with the help of other prisoners, but who can he trust, and can they trust him?

Cast

Peter Wyngarde (*Number Two*), Ronald Radd (*Rook*), Rosalie Crutchley (*Queen*), George Coulouris (*Man with the Stick*), Patricia Jessel (*1st Psychiatrist*), Bee Duffell (*2nd Psychiatrist*), Basil Dignam (*Supervisor*), Danvers Walker (*Painter*), Denis Shaw (*Shopkeeper*), Victor Platt (*Assistant Supervisor*), Shivaun O'Casey (*Nurse*), Geoffrey Reed (*Skipper*), Terence Donovan (*Sailor*), Joe Dunne, Romo Gorrara (*Tower Guards*), Jimmy Millar** (*Escapee*), Glyn Jones** (*Electrician*), Cynthia Jones** (*White Queen*), John O'Connor** (*Gardener*)

Information

- The episode was originally titled 'The Queen's Pawn'.
- Writer Gerald Kelsey was inspired to include a human chess match in the episode after seeing such a game being played in Germany.

Hammer Into Anvil

Written by Roger Woddis
Directed by Pat Jackson

First UK Transmission: 1st December 1967

When a young female Villager commits suicide after an interrogation by Number Two, Number Six is determined to avenge her death.

Cast

Patrick Cargill (*Number Two*), Basil Hoskins (*Number 14*), Victor Maddern (*Band Master*), Norman Scace (*Psychiatric Director*), Peter Swanwick (*Supervisor*), Derek Aylward (*New Supervisor*), Hilary Dwyer (*Number 73*), Arthur Gross (*Control Room Operator*), Victor Woolf (*Shop Assistant*), Michael Segal (*Laboratory Technician*), Margo Andrew (*Shop Kiosk Girl*), Susan Sheers (*Female Code Expert*), Jackie Cooper, Fred Haggerty, Eddie Powell, George Leech (*Guardians*)

Information

- Patrick Cargill's emotional closing scene was the first to be filmed for this episode.
- The bizarre trampoline fighting sport first seen in this episode is called Kosho, and was devised by Patrick McGoohan.

Checkmate - Anyone for Chess?

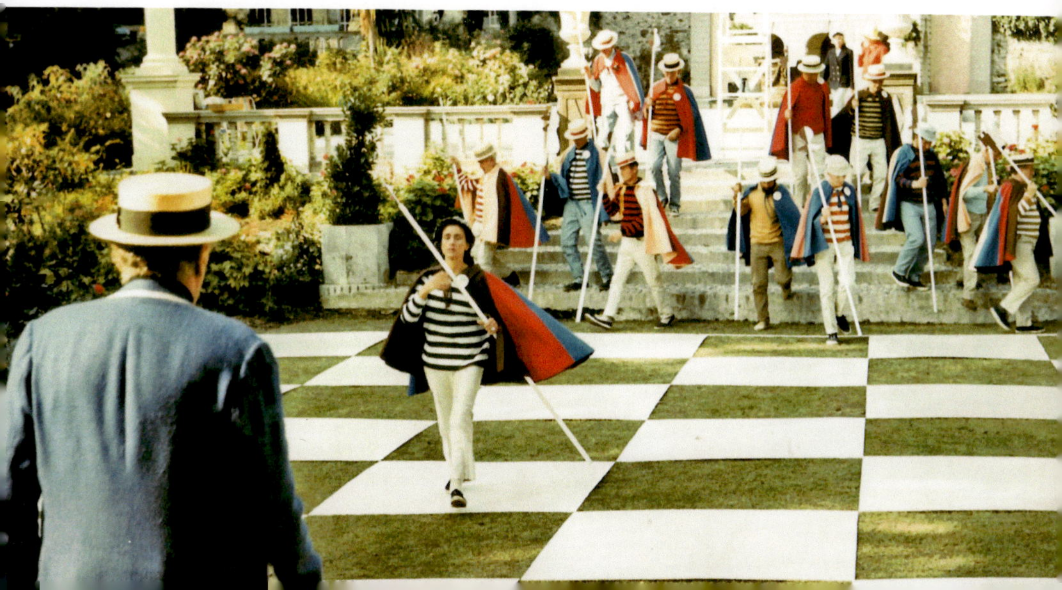

It's Your Funeral

Written by Michael Cramoy
Directed by Robert Asher

First UK Transmission: 8th December 1967

Number Six learns of a plot to assassinate the retiring Number Two, but finds that he and his young ally are not being believed and must work alone to stop the killing.

Cast

Derren Nesbitt (*New Number Two*), André Van Gyseghem (*Retiring Number Two*), Annette Andre (*Watchmaker's Daughter*), Mark Eden (*Number 100*), Martin Miller (*Watchmaker*), Wanda Ventham (*Computer Attendant*), Mark Burns (*Number Two's Assistant*), Peter Swanwick (*Supervisor*), Charles Lloyd Pack (*Artist*), Grace Arnold (*Number 36*), Arthur White (*Stall-Holder*), Michael Bilton (*MC Councillor*), Gerry Crampton (*Kosho Opponent*)

Information

- Number 100 was to have been killed by Rover. Shots were filmed, but cut and used in *Arrival*; glimpses of Mark Eden's distinctive pink blazer feature in that episode's Rover attack.

- Director Robert Asher left the production early after being criticised by McGoohan on set in front of the cast and crew. McGoohan directed the rest of the episode himself.

A Change of Mind

Written by Roger Parkes
Directed by Patrick McGoohan

First UK Transmission: 15th December 1967

When Number Six refuses to conform, he is branded 'Unmutual' by The Village and must undergo brain surgery to cure him of his individuality.

Cast

John Sharp (*Number Two*), Angela Browne (*Number 86*), George Pravda (*Doctor*), Kathleen Breck (*Number 42*), Peter Swanwick (*Supervisor*), Thomas Heathcote (*Lobo Man*), Bartlett Mullins (*Committee Chairman*), Michael Miller (*Number 93*), Joseph Cuby, Michael Chow (*Members of Social Group*), June Ellis (*Number 48*), John Hamblin, Michael Billington (*Woodland Men*)

Information

- McGoohan directed this episode himself after the original director Roy Rossotti was sacked on his first day in the role.

- Actor John Sharp was cast as Number Two, but a production office error led to him being screen-credited as John Sharpe.

It's Your Funeral - Preventing Assassination

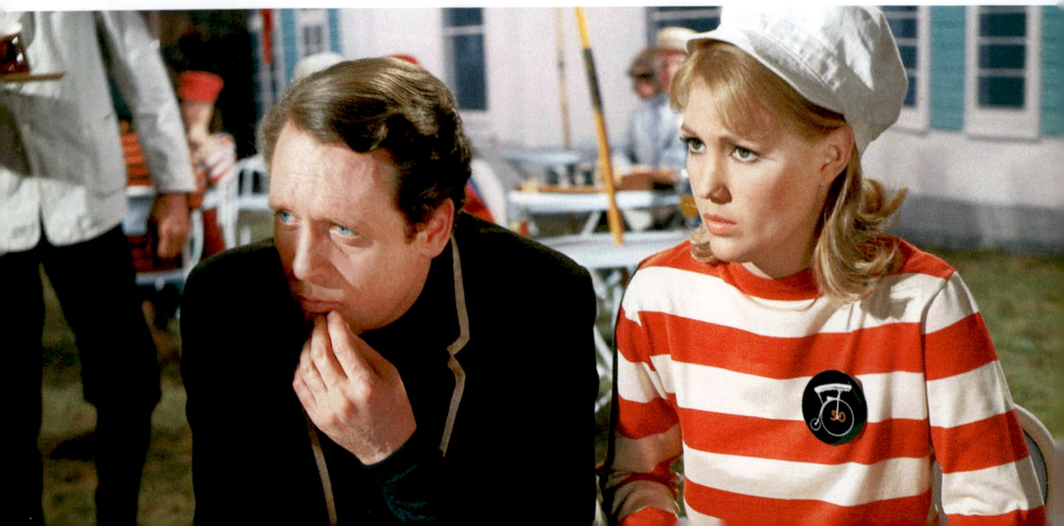

Do Not Forsake Me Oh My Darling

Written by Vincent Tilsley
Directed by Pat Jackson

First UK Transmission: 22nd December 1967

Number Six's mind is placed inside the body of another man, and only Professor Seltzman can change it back. But where is the Professor, and will Number Six find him before The Village or his former bosses do?

Cast

Clifford Evans (*Number Two*), Zena Walker (*Janet*), Nigel Stock (*The Colonel*), Hugo Schuster (*Seltzman*), John Wentworth (*Sir Charles*), James Bree (*Villiers*), Lloyd Lamble (*Stapleton*), Patrick Jordan (*Danvers*), Lockwood West (*Camera Shop Manager*), Frederic Abbott (*Potter*), Gertan Klauber (*Café Waiter*), Henry Longhurst* (*Old Guest*), Danvers Walker* (*First New Man*), John Nolan (*Young Guest*), William Lyon Brown** (*Undertaker*)

Information

- Patrick McGoohan was absent for much of the filming, making *Ice Station Zebra* for MGM.
- The episode was originally titled 'Face Unknown', and was heavily re-written, much to the annoyance of writer Vincent Tilsley.
- As Nigel Stock couldn't drive, stock footage of McGoohan driving around London was used, with Stock filmed against back projection.

The Clues Are There!

Whilst Portmeirion was deliberately chosen as a location due to its mix of styles, meaning the viewer would not know where the series was set, there are several on-screen clues to the location, including 'Portmeirion Road' being used as Seltzman's address in *Do Not Forsake Me Oh My Darling*, and the use of Portmeirion Pottery in The Village.

Living in Harmony

Written by David Tomblin & Ian Rakoff
Directed by David Tomblin

First UK Transmission: 29th December 1967

In a Wild West setting, Number Six resigns his job as sheriff, but he cannot escape from the town of Harmony and learns that he needs to kill to survive.

Cast

Alexis Kanner (*The Kid*), David Bauer (*The Judge*), Valerie French (*Kathy*), George Tanner (*Town Elder*), Gordon Sterne (*Bystander*), Michael Balfour (*Will*), Larry Taylor (*Mexican Sam*), Monti de Lyle (*Town Dignitary*), Douglas Jones (*Horse Dealer*), Bill Nick, Les Crawford, Frank Maher (*Gunmen*), Max Faulkner, Bill Cummings, Eddie Eddon (*Horsemen*), Peter Brace** (*Zeke*), Peter Brayham** (*Thug*), Gary Maher** (*Boy*)

Information

- The episode was devised by assistant editor Ian Rakoff, inspired by a Gene Autry comic.
- *Living in Harmony* was originally titled 'Do Not Forsake Me Oh My Darling', a title which was of course recycled for another episode.
- This is the only *Prisoner* episode in which Frank Maher, McGoohan's stunt and second unit double for the entire series, is given a credited part (that of 3rd Gunman).

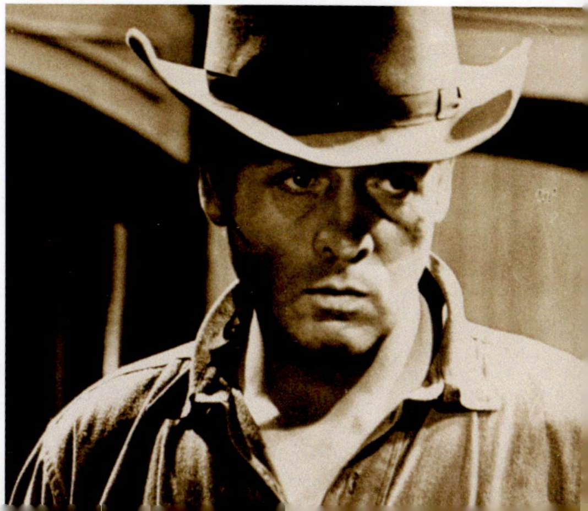

Living in Harmony - Harmony's new sheriff

The Girl Who Was Death

Written by Terence Feely
Directed by David Tomblin

First UK Transmission: 18th January 1968 †

Number Six is in disguise, hot on the heels of a mad scientist hell-bent on destroying London, but on his tail at every turn is a mysterious girl who wants him dead.

Cast

Kenneth Griffith (*Schnipps*), Justine Lord (*Sonia*), Christopher Benjamin (*Potter*), Michael Brennan (*Killer Karminski*), Harold Berens (*Boxing MC*), Sheena Marsh (*Barmaid*), Max Faulkner, John Rees, Joe Gladwin, Jimmy Millar** (*Napoleons*), John Drake (*Bowler*), Gaynor Steward (*Little Girl*), Graham Steward, Stephen Howe (*Little Boys*), Alexis Kanner** (*Photographer*), George McGrath** (*Hawke-Englishe*)

Information

- Terence Feely's script was based on an unused *Danger Man* storyline by David Tomblin.
- At an early stage in development, the Napoleon character was to be Adolf Hitler.

† Episode aired on Scottish Television one day before ATV Midlands transmission.

Once Upon a Time

Written by Patrick McGoohan
Directed by Patrick McGoohan

First UK Transmission: 25th January 1968 †

Number Six is regressed back into his childhood and must face the ultimate test of Degree Absolute against a familiar Number Two, with freedom for the winner and death for the loser.

Cast

Leo McKern (*Number Two*), Peter Swanwick (*Supervisor*), John Cazabon (*Umbrella Man*), John Maxim* (*Number 86*)

Information

- *Once Upon a Time* was originally written by McGoohan as 'Degree Absolute', under the pseudonym of Archibald Schwartz.
- Despite being the 16th episode screened, *Once Upon a Time* was actually the 6th to be filmed.
- Leo McKern suffered a nervous breakdown during the filming of this intense episode.

† Episode aired on Scottish Television one day before ATV Midlands transmission.

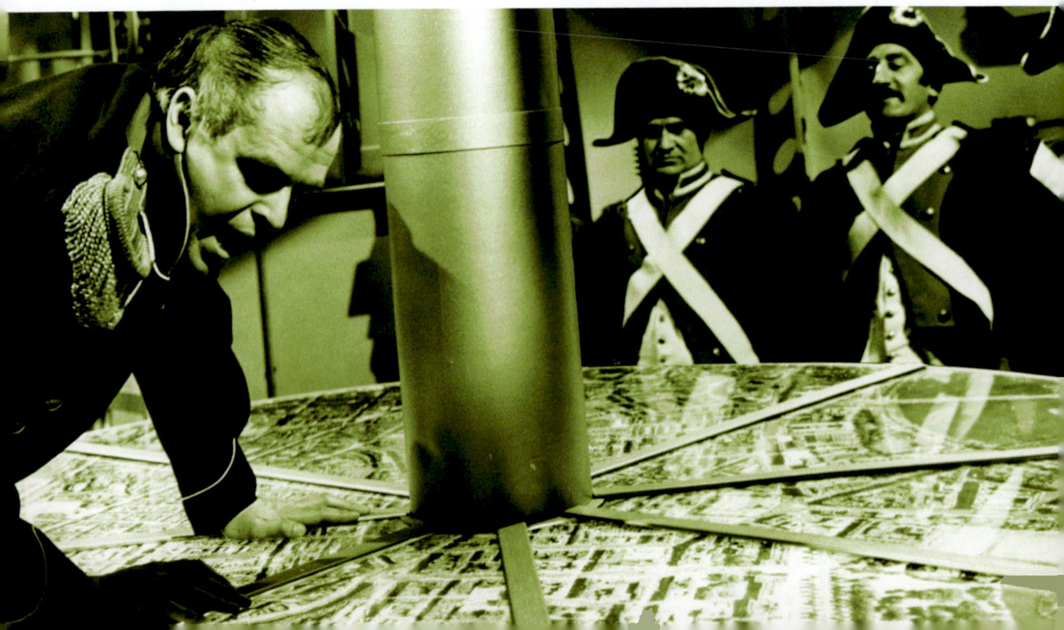

The Girl Who Was Death - Target: London!

Fall Out

Written by Patrick McGoohan
Directed by Patrick McGoohan

First UK Transmission: 1st February 1968 †

Number Six has earned the right to be an individual, and to come face to face with Number One, but with freedom within his grasp is all as it seems?

Cast

Leo McKern (*Number Two*), Alexis Kanner (*Number 48*), Kenneth Griffith (*The President*), Peter Swanwick (*Supervisor*), Michael Miller (*The Delegate*), Graham Nearn** (*Seven Driver*), Roy Beck** (*Number One*), Frank Forsyth** (*Driver*)

Information

- The Beatles track *All You Need is Love* was chosen for the episode by music editor Eric Mival. Everyman Films paid the princely sum of £60 to use the track in perpetuity.

- The cavern set was so large that it took up two sound stages at MGM studios.

† Episode aired on Scottish Television one day before ATV Midlands transmission.

Series Production Credits

Patrick McGoohan (*Executive Producer*), David Tomblin (*Producer*), George Markstein (*Script Editor*), Brendan J Stafford BSC (*Director of Photography*), Jack Shampan (*Art Director*), Rose Tobias Shaw (*Casting Director*), Ron Grainer (*Theme*), Albert Elms (*Musical Director*), Bernard Williams, Ronald Liles (*Production Managers*), Gino Marotta, Ernie Morris, Ernie Lewis (*Assistant Directors*), Jack Lowin, Len Harris, Bob Kindred (*Camera Operators*), Robert Monks (*2nd Unit Camera*), John Bramall, Cyril Swern (*Sound Recordists*), Frank Maher (*Stunt Arranger*), Jackie Cooper (*Fight Arranger*), Doris Martin, Josie Fulford, Ann Besserman, Phyllis Townshend (*Continuity*), Kenneth Bridgeman, Colin Southcott, John Lageu (*Set Dressers*), Eddie Knight, Frank Turner (*Make-Up*), Pat McDermot, Olive Mills (*Hairdressing*), Masada Wilmot, Dora Lloyd (*Wardrobe*), Lee Doig, Spencer Reeve, Geoffrey Foot GBFE, John S Smith, Eric Boyd-Perkins GBFE, Noreen Ackland GBFE (*Editors*), Wilf Thompson, Peter Elliott, Ken Rolls, Stanley Smith, Clive Smith (*Sound Editors*), Bob Dearberg, Eric Mival, John S Smith (*Music Editors*)

An ITC Production
by Everyman Films Limited

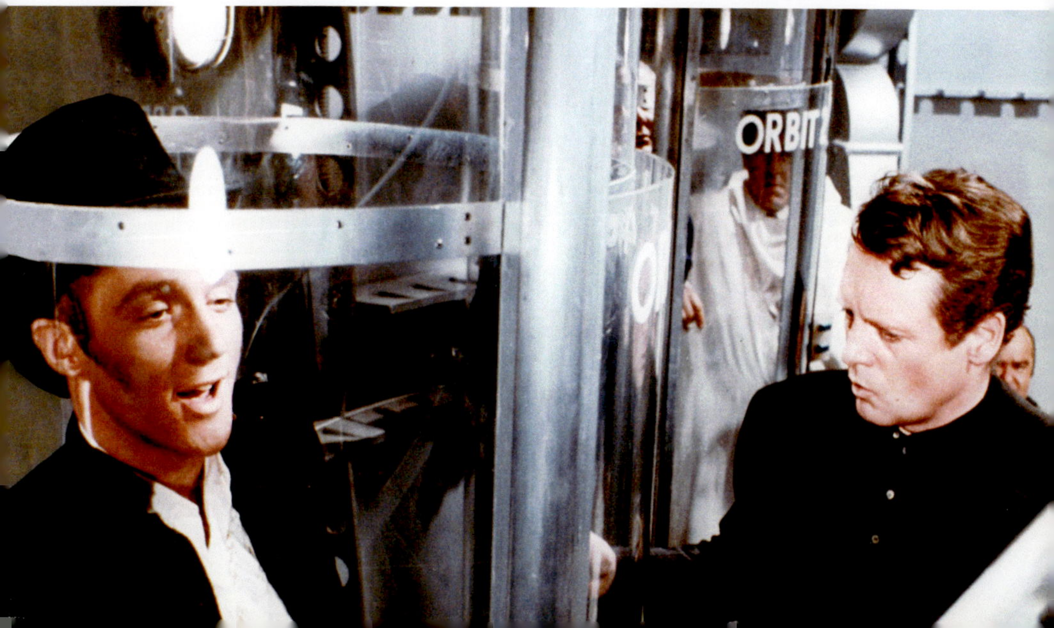

Fall Out - Kanner and McGoohan
© QML

What's It All About?

"If I gave all the answers you would no longer have a role when watching it."
Patrick McGoohan, *The Observer*, 1991

The Prisoner is unique as a television spectacle in that it asked more questions than perhaps it answered – and challenged viewers to think for themselves, rather than be force-fed the conclusions.

Fans and academics have been studying the series in the decades since *The Prisoner*'s first screening, with books and magazines produced on almost a monthly basis, and a number of university courses founded to examine its meanings.

For those of you who have not seen the series fully, I will not spoil the surprises for you, but here are some of the most commonly asked questions:

Why the Penny Farthing as the symbol of The Village?
Patrick McGoohan stated that the bicycle was an ironic symbol of progress: "I think we are progressing too fast. I think we should pull back." The canopy, he stated, was "for protection."

Original Villager Badge

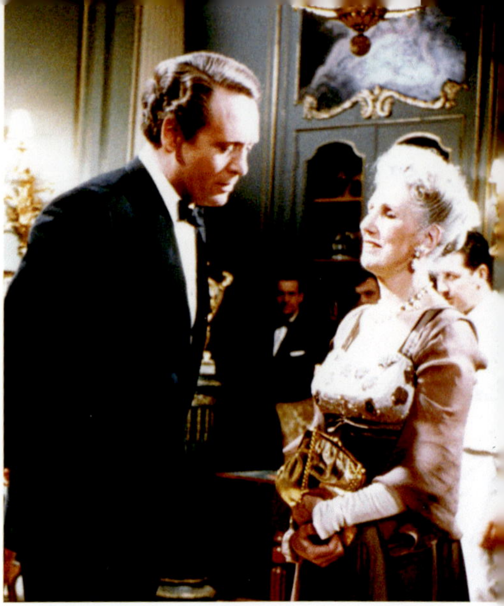

A.B. and C. - Six in Drake's clothing?

Is Number Six John Drake from *Danger Man*?
Patrick McGoohan always maintained, in public at least, that the two characters were not the same. Number Six was 'Everyman', representing each and every one of us, in that we are all Prisoners in one way or another. McGoohan also stated that Number Six could just as easily be a scientist as he could a spy, and that John Drake would have escaped a lot more easily than Number Six managed to do, were he to be placed in The Village.

However, George Markstein felt that the two characters were the same, and it was only due to the issue of royalties needing to be paid to Drake's creator Ralph Smart that the character was never named as Drake. Several crew members believed it was Drake, including Frank Maher and Tony Sloman, who state they were told by McGoohan privately that the two characters were the same.

It could be said that *The Prisoner* is also autobiographical of McGoohan, who resigned from *Danger Man* to make the series. Peter Graham Scott worked on this basis when directing *The General*.

In *Many Happy Returns* Number Six's name is given as Peter Smith. Was he giving a false name, or did it have to be his real name as he was trying to prove he owned the house he was in?

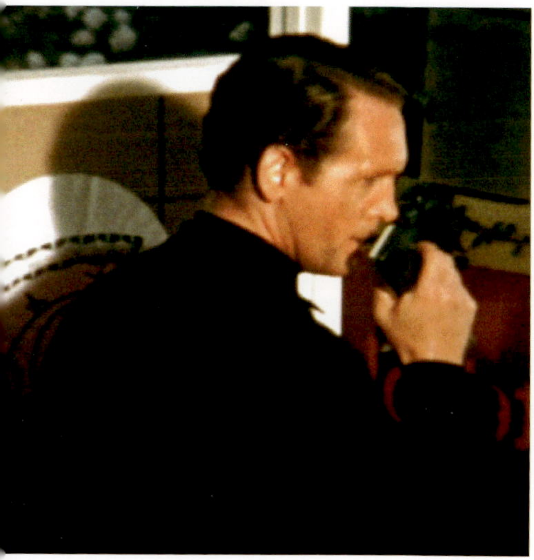

No number, no call...
© Rick Davy

Why Number Six?
Patrick McGoohan said that the number was chosen as it was the only integer that becomes another when turned upside down. George Markstein stated that being numbered '6' implied that the character was important, but not high enough in rank to be in a position of authority.

Which side runs The Village?
There is no definitive answer to this. In both *Many Happy Returns* and *Do Not Forsake Me Oh My Darling* Number Six seemingly returns to The Village against the will or knowledge of his former employers. However, it is clear that many of his old colleagues, such as those seen in *Arrival* and *The Chimes of Big Ben*, have either swapped sides or help run The Village.

What is the strange 'Be Seeing You' salute?
The symbol is that which Christians used to make, the sign of the fish. Patrick McGoohan had used the phrase 'Be Seeing You' several times previously in *Danger Man* and felt it would be an interesting – and sinister – addition to The Village, with everyone under constant surveillance.

What does it all mean?
Quite simply, *The Prisoner* is an allegory. The Village represents society, and the series' themes are just as relevant today as they were in the 1960s, if not more so. The Village is all around us, and we are all prisoners of ourselves. Be Seeing You!

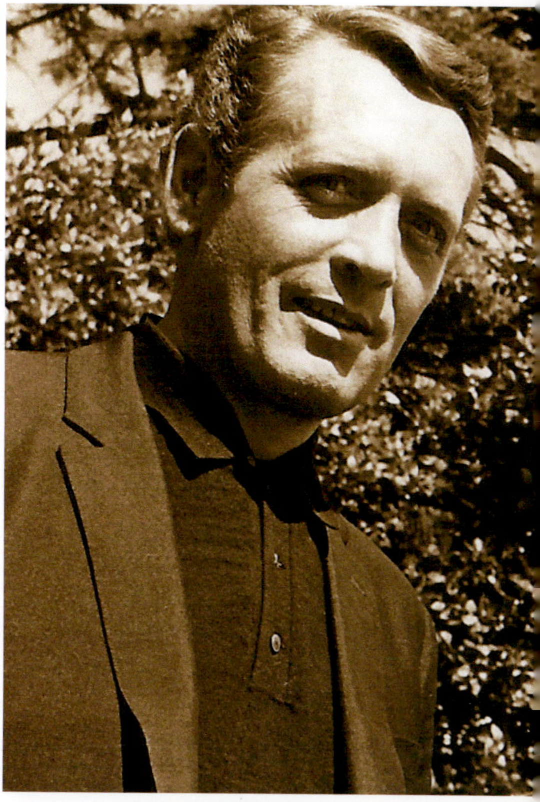

Patrick McGoohan
© Y Cymro / Leri Roberts

Brought to Book

The Prisoner has probably been discussed and analysed more than any other television show, with well over fifty books written about it since 1967.

Shortly after transmission, a trio of novels based on *The Prisoner* were published (with further novels from Powys Media issued in the early 2000s), and throughout the late 1970s and 1980s a succession of fan-produced publications kept the series alive.

The first officially sanctioned book, *The Prisoner Companion* (White/Ali, 1988), was criticised by Patrick McGoohan and fans alike due to its inaccuracies, so it was not until the publication, first in France and then the UK, of *The Prisoner* (Carrazé/Oswald, 1989) that the series could boast its first popular coffee-table style book, filled with lavish photographs.

All manner of production and episode guides followed over the next fifteen years, with Robert Fairclough's trio of books (*The Official Companion*, and two volumes of *The Original Scripts*) regarded as the best researched and most interesting of the larger sized books to have been published. Whilst out of print, copies can be regularly found on online book and auction sites.

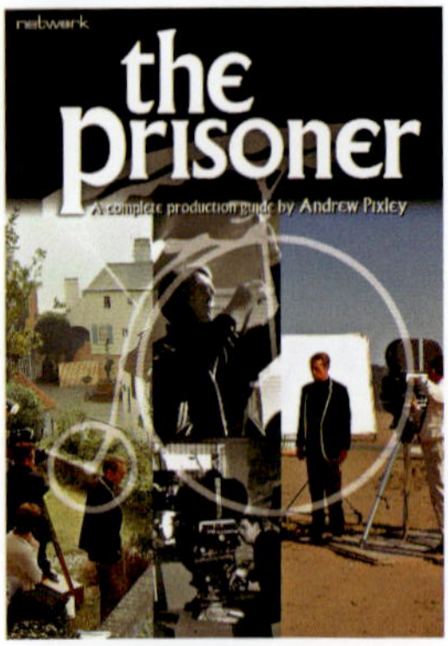

In 2007 Andrew Pixley's *The Prisoner: A Complete Production Guide*, included with Network's 40th anniversary Blu-ray and DVD sets, raised the bar even higher in terms of the presentation of detailed production information.

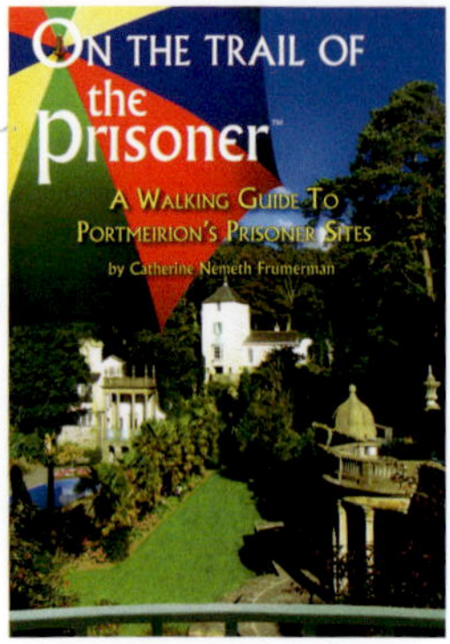

On the Trail of The Prisoner: A Walking Guide to Portmeirion's Prisoner Sites (Frumerman, 2003) provides fans of both *The Prisoner* and Portmeirion with a handy guide to The Village's *Prisoner* filming locations, and *George Markstein and The Prisoner* (ed. Roger Goodman, 2014) provides information on the life of the series' script editor. Both are available from Portmeirion and online *Prisoner* and book sites.

Two biographies of Patrick McGoohan have been written, and two crew members, assistant editor Ian Rakoff and music editor Eric Mival, have written autobiographical memoirs of their time on the series. Whilst Rakoff's *Inside the Prisoner* is now out of print, Mival's *Cutting Edge: My Life in Film and Television* (2016) is available from Portmeirion and quoitmedia.co.uk.

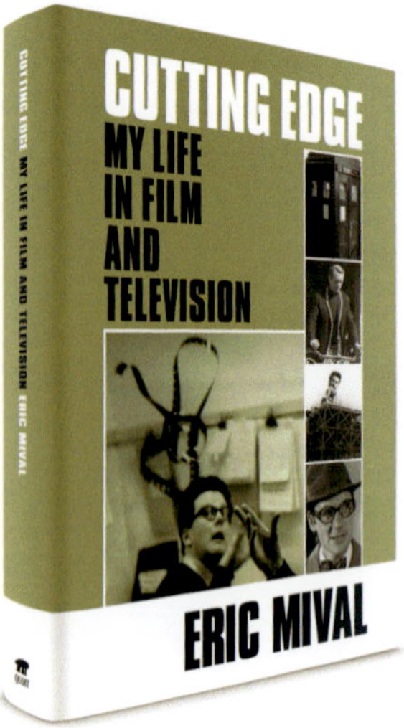

Sound and Vision

Thanks to Network, *The Prisoner*'s 17 episodes are now available for us to watch on beautiful high definition Blu-ray and on DVD, but this wasn't always the case.

The first commercial release of *The Prisoner* on video did not occur until 1982, when Precision Video Limited released four cassettes, each containing two episodes edited together into a 'movie' format. The company did not complete the full run of episodes, stopping at eight.

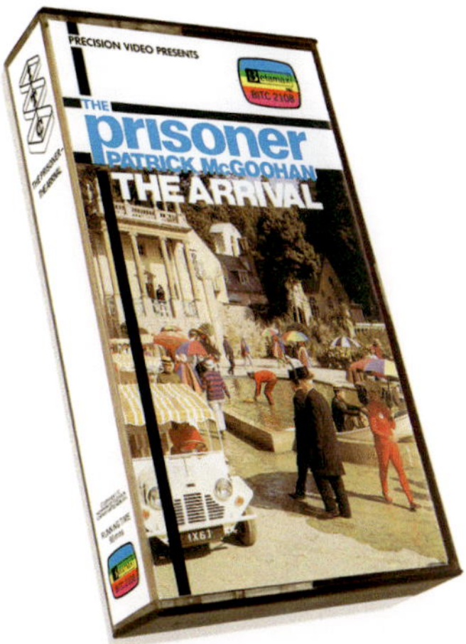

The first full release of the series on video came in 1986 from Channel 5 Video, and several more releases, including a full issue on the LaserDisc format, followed. In 2000, Carlton released the series for the first time on DVD, with A&E following suit in North America later the same year. Carlton subsequently issued the *35th Anniversary Prisoner Companion* in 2002, which included an alternative cut of *Arrival*.

In 2003 Umbrella Entertainment in Australia released their DVD set, which included a number of bonus features, and in 2005 DeAgostini issued the episodes fortnightly as part of a magazine partwork series.

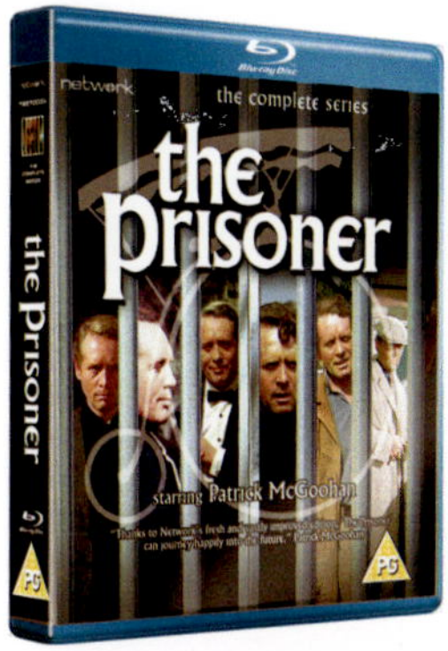

In 2007 Network went back to the original film elements for their stunning high definition 40th anniversary set, which included the feature-length *Don't Knock Yourself Out* documentary. Blu-rays and DVDs of this edition are available to buy from Portmeirion and networkonair.com.

Some of the series' soundtrack music has also been released. A variation of Ron Grainer's theme music was released by RCA in 1967 as a 7-inch vinyl single.

In 1987 a gatefold vinyl soundtrack compilation of incidental and theme music was released by Bam Caruso records, followed in the 1990s by a series of audio CDs, cassettes, and vinyl releases of music highlights from Silva Screen.

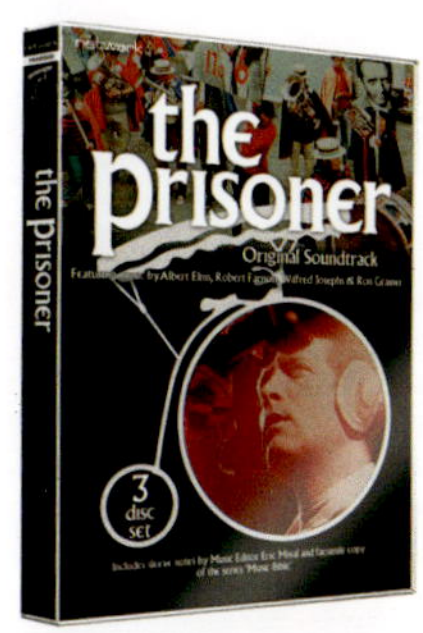

All the music (apart from the songs by The Beatles, Carmen Miranda and The Four Lads, which appear in *Fall Out*) is now available on two 3-CD sets. The music specially composed for the series can be purchased from networkonair.com, while the Chappell Library music cues from the series are collected together in a separate set from theunmutual.co.uk.

In 2015 Network also released highlights from the series' music on limited edition gatefold black and white vinyl LPs.

The Legacy of The Prisoner

When *The Prisoner* finished its debut run in February 1968, ATV's switchboard was jammed with calls from angry and confused viewers, who had expected a Bond-style 'all will be revealed' ending.

Whilst reviews were mixed, the series certainly captured the imagination of large swathes of viewers and had a profound impact on many of those watching.

Following some repeat runs of the series across various regions of ITV in the 1970s, in 1977 the first fan club, Six of One, was established, and others such as Once Upon a Time followed. In more recent years internet sites such as theunmutual.co.uk have kept fans updated with the latest news, research and events related to the series.

There have been many attempts to remake *The Prisoner*. Patrick McGoohan, who felt that the series would have worked better as a seven-episode mini-series, was among those who tried to revive it. In 2009 an ITV/AMC co-production of *The Prisoner*, starring Jim Caviezel and Ian McKellen, was screened to poor reviews.

A much better received re-imagining of the series came in 2015, when Nicholas Briggs of bigfinish.com debuted a *Prisoner* audio drama series, starring Mark Elstob as Number Six. In 2017 *Everyman*, Brian Gorman's one-man stage show detailing the life of Patrick McGoohan, was adapted for both graphic novel and audio CD formats, available from quoitmedia.co.uk.

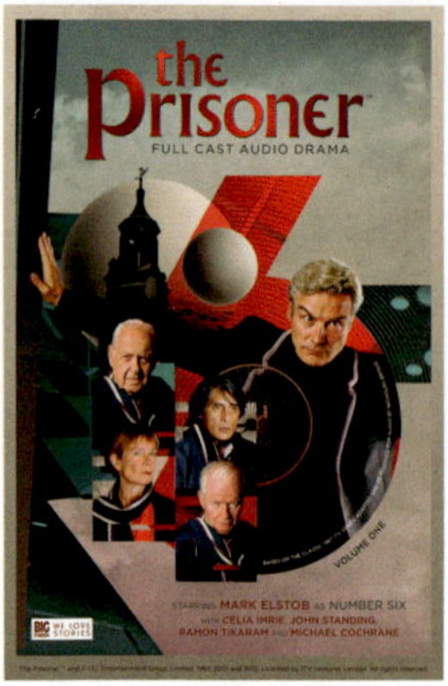

In the half-century since the series first aired, creators of many films and television shows, such as *Lost* and *Twin Peaks*, have cited *The Prisoner* as an influence on their work. Pop and rock bands such as Dr Feelgood, Mansun and Iron Maiden have used *Prisoner* imagery in songs, videos, and album covers, and the series and Portmeirion have attracted many celebrity admirers, such as The Beatles, Stephen Fry, Jools Holland and countless others.

Likewise, Portmeirion is now a popular place for TV shows and films to be made, thanks largely to *The Prisoner*.

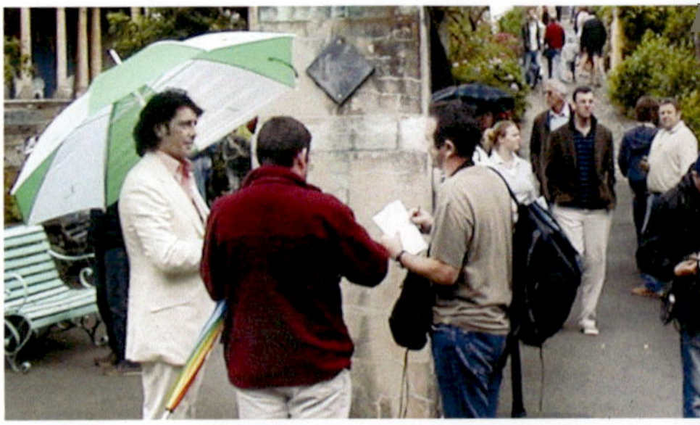

Laurence Llewellyn-Bowen at Portmeirion
© Rick Davy

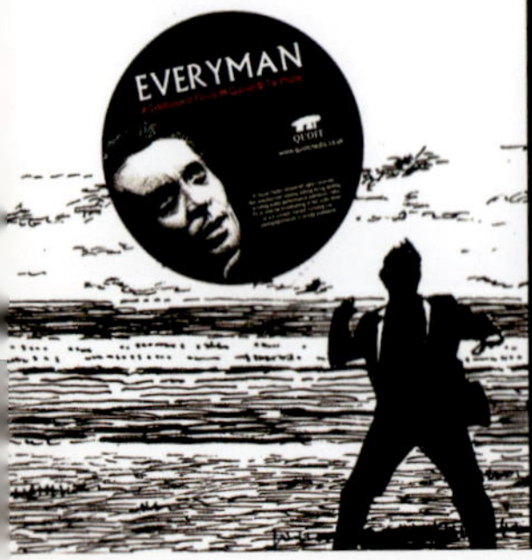

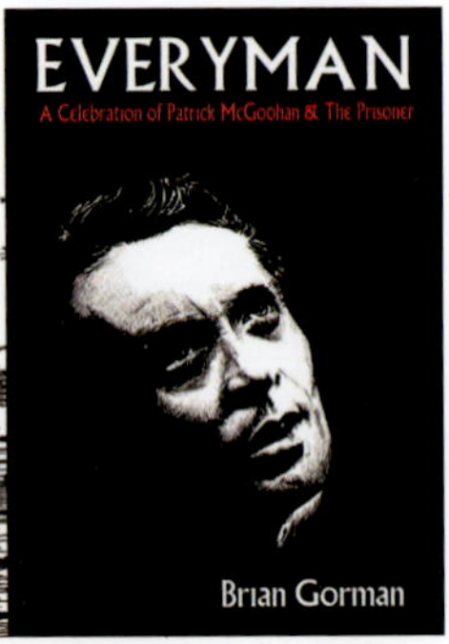

Whilst not everyone was satisfied with what they saw in February 1968, Patrick McGoohan certainly achieved what he set out to do: send a valuable message to and about society, and get people talking. Not before or since has a television programme managed to do both to such an extent.